B.O.S.S.

MOVES

Business Optimization
Success Secrets from a
Million Dollar Round Table

MYRON GOLDEN, PH.D.

B.O.S.S. MOVES

Business Optimization Success Secrets from a Million Dollar Round Table

All Scripture quotations, unless otherwise noted, are from the King James Version of the Bible.

Skillionaire Enterprises, LLC
27251 Wesley Chapel Blvd #1040
Wesley Chapel, FL 33544-4285

For permission requests, speaking inquiries, and bulk order purchase options, email connect@myrongolden.com.

ISBN: 978-1-7378562-0-7

Interior Design by Transcendent Publishing

Cover and Graphic Design by Ariel Elise

Edited by Lori Lynn Enterprises

Disclaimer: The author in no way, shape, or form considers any of the information in this book to be advice, promise, guarantee, warranty, or any form of professional advice. It is intended for informational and educational purposes only. The results produced by the author or anyone referenced in the book are mentioned for illustration purposes only and are not intended to imply or suggest that you will have results that are at all similar to those in the book.

Printed in the United States of America.

"In all labour there is profit: but the talk of the lips tendeth only to penury. The crown of the wise is their riches: but the foolishness of fools is folly."

—Proverbs 14:23-24

CONTENTS

DEDICATION

It is with great joy that I dedicate this book to all the entrepreneurs who have been stuck on the struggle bus of building a business for longer than they would like. Some have been stuck for six months while others have been stuck for six years. If you have been wracking your brain to figure out how to break through to 6 or 7 figures per year or 6 or 7 figures per month, you may find this book to be the most important business book of your life.

The reason I wrote this book for you is because I *was* you. I was you not just for a month or for a year—I was just like you for decades, seeking but not finding.

When I finally had my breakthrough (which I tell you about in this book), I was blown away! I was blown away by how much I made. I was blown away by how fast I made it. And I was blown away by how simple and easy it was for me to make more in a week than I had ever made in a month.

I decided at that moment that I would spend the rest of my life teaching entrepreneurs how to create wealth. I've written books on financial literacy. I've conducted seminars on how to scale businesses. And I've created coaching programs to assist entrepreneurs as they become the kind of people who can create massive wealth and free time.

If I have just described you, I want you to know the love, respect, and admiration I have for you and your family because you had the courage to take on this mantle! If you will read this book, study it, and internalize it, I promise you can trust the principles to be faithful. Not only will you have a chance at success that you may have never had before, but you will also become a person you didn't know you could become.

I hope this book serves as a source of inspiration and illumination for you that fills your heart with energy and your mind with clarity as you go out and change the world through your mission, your calling, your ministry, which others will see as your business.

As I dedicate this book to you, I challenge you to never give up on your dream. Never settle for less than your best. Never see any obstacle as bigger than you. Never see any enemy as stronger than you. And if you forget everything else I've said above, remember, I believe in you!

FOREWORD

The first time I heard Myron speak was at a small master-mind group almost a decade ago. He wasn't there as a speaker but as an attendee. During one of the sessions, he had some wisdom to share, and he stood up, walked to the whiteboard, and in about five minutes, quickly mapped out a strategy that he had discovered to increase his sales.

All of us in the room that day watched in amazement at the power of what he shared. I quickly took some notes, and that one nugget that he shared that day has gone on to make me a small fortune over the past 10 years.

After that experience, Myron and I had a chance to become friends. Each time we talked over the years, he would say things in passing that were so profound, I would have to stop what I was doing and figure out a way to document it for myself. Sometimes they turned into podcast episodes, many other times I asked him to do full sessions at our live events so that the people that I've been called to serve could learn these principles directly from Myron.

Now, Myron is a self-described "chill-ionaire" who likes to make a lot of money, but not at the expense of trading it for his time. As you will read about in the chapters that follow, he's a big believer in creating high-profit, high-margin products, meaning most of the things he sells start at $35,000–$50,000 or more!

While I am a big believer that everything he creates is worth AT LEAST 10X the investment (and in most cases a LOT more), this high-ticket price has kept these secrets from the masses.

Over the years, I've literally begged Myron to figure out a way to share these strategies with more people, and I'm SO excited that he's finally put them into a book that is accessible to everyone! This is a book that I will share with my kids, with my coaching students, and one that I will refer to over and over again as I continue to progress throughout my life.

This is a book that you should read if you are starting a business and you want to save yourself years of trial and error as it gives you the actual shortcuts to success. If you have an existing business, but you're trying to figure out how to break the false beliefs that are keeping you from where you want to go, then this book is for you. And if you're happy with your business, but you're trying to figure out how to create an actual legacy, this book will serve as a roadmap that will show you how to create a legacy that endures past yourself.

I'm grateful that Myron wrote this book, and I hope that you love it as much as I do!

—**Russell Brunson**
New York Times Bestselling Author
Co-Founder of ClickFunnels

INTRODUCTION

B.O.S.S. Moves: These are the moves you'll be making once you become a B.O.S.S. (Business Optimization Success Strategist) who has learned the Business Optimization Success Secrets (B.O.S.S.) that I teach in this book.

In 2020 at Funnel Hacking Live (a business sales and marketing conference with over 4,000 people), I had the privilege of hosting a roundtable discussion with business owners from all over the world. I decided that I would spend those two hours teaching them what I have taught my high-level clients—strategies that have helped them make millions of dollars in their respective businesses.

If those business owners would have hired me for a business growth coaching session and paid my $25,000-per-hour fee, what I shared at that round table is what I would have shared with them. They would have paid $50,000 for that very same content. Now I am going to share those same principles with you in the pages of this book.

This book is not full of some rehashed copycat business slogans that I got secondhand from someone else. Not at all. This book is filled with principles that I have discovered while doing thousands of business transactions to the tune of millions of dollars.

In the pages that follow, I will do everything in my power to help you discover the simplicity and elegance of optimizing a business exponentially to whatever level you desire. I think you would have to agree that if I can't do that, it wouldn't be very smart for me to make such a bold promise in the introduction of this book.

So can we agree to begin with the premise that my above statement is either true or not true? If it's not true, it won't take you very many pages to figure out that I'm pontificating at best. But if I am indeed telling you the truth, then your life will never be the same.

It is my belief that if you are going to take on the risks and challenges of starting, sustaining, and scaling a business, you aren't doing all of that just to make money. You are taking on this huge task because you desire to create real wealth. I'm talking about the kind of wealth that changes your family for generations. That is what has happened for me. And it is my desire that you will experience a transformation of similar magnitude.

Regardless of whether you are a business owner who stepped onto the business landscape and experienced immediate success or whether you are an entrepreneur who has been on the "struggle bus" of business for years, you will find the principles in this book extremely beneficial.

So, allow me to tell you about the week that changed the game for me. It was April 1999, which was the year after the best financial year of my life. After growing up poor and the second of seven brothers, I started working at age 14 for a mere $1.55 per hour in my first summer job. By 1998, I was 37 years old and I had just made a whopping $48,000 that year (which is an average of about $4,000 per month).

Back to the story: In April of 1999, I accidentally made $6,200 in one week. That's right, I made more in a week than I had ever made in a month. This was the experience that changed my life. That's when the light bulb came on. My first thought was, *Wow, that was easy*. Then, I thought this must mean that:

It's easier to make a lot of money in a short period of time than it is to make a little money over a long period of time.

I decided from that time on, I would only look for easier ways to make a lot. That was one of the most important financial decisions of my life.

It's amazing how we as human beings are great at finding what we're looking for. I shifted my focus in January, and by April, I had a $6,200 week. By July of that same year, I had my first $8,000 day. By then I felt like I was starting to gain some momentum.

Because of that breakthrough, I decided that all of the money and financial slogans that I had heard my entire life about money were bogus and not worth believing anymore. I just flushed them down the drain. I threw them all out.

I thought, *I don't believe that time is money anymore. I don't believe in a hard day's work for a hard day's pay. I don't believe in eight hours of work for eight hours of pay, whatever that means.*

I just believe it's easier to make a lot of money in a short period of time than it is to make a little money over a long period of time. After all, the people who were making 100 times more money than me weren't working 100 times harder or 100 times more hours, so it had to be something else.

We are paid for the level of value that we bring into the world. The level of value is what matters. Not how hard we work to create that value. Not even what value we bring in the world, but for the level of value we bring. That's the level at which we're compensated. I will cover this in great detail later.

When I came to that realization, I started focusing on and leveling up to only offer higher and higher levels of value. And that's when everything changed.

I went from driving a trash truck for $6.25 an hour (the first job I had after I got married) to building a business that does 6 and sometimes even 7 figures per month. And as crazy as it may sound, sometimes we even have 6- and 7-figure days.

The business growth principles that we've discovered not only work in our own business, but they also work just as well for our clients. We have many clients who have earned $100K Day awards and we even have clients who have earned our coveted "Million Dollar Day" award.

When I think about the fact that there was a time when I told my young wife, who I had made a lot of promises to, that if I can get enough overtime, we can make $300 a week. And if we can make $300 a week, we're going to be okay. Our rent was $250 a month. Our car payment was about $144 a month. We had insurance and utilities and food and stuff, but I thought that if we could make $300 a week, we're going to be great. That was as big as my vision was because I had bought into all the lies that I had been told about money my whole life.

There are times now in my life where I make more money in an hour than I used to make in an entire decade. And it's all because I shifted my focus.

> **When you shift your focus,
> what you see will change.**

Focus is more important than what's there. Think about it, even with a camera, sometimes when you have a really good camera lens and you focus in on one thing, it makes everything else blurry.

I submit to you that when you shift your mind and start focusing on things that make the biggest difference, the things that make the least amount of difference will become invisible to you. Just like when you are focused on those things that make a little difference, the things that would make a big difference are out of focus and you can't really see them.

If you can't see them, it's like they're not there.

In this book, I lay out principle upon principle about how you can shift your focus to the things that can make the biggest difference. When you do this, you will offer value at a higher level. And that's when you'll start making a lot of money in your business in a short period of time instead of a little money over a long period of time. Enjoy.

SECTION I

Three B.O.S.S. Moves
That Make All the
Difference

IF YOU WANT TO SCALE FAST, FOCUS ON THIS FIRST

There are three B.O.S.S. moves that make all the difference in whether a business is successful or not. If you get these three moves right, you greatly increase your chances of success. If you get them wrong, you almost guarantee imminent failure. If you get this right, your business will make a lot of money in a short period of time. If you get it wrong, your business will struggle and ultimately die a painful death that could leave you financially and emotionally devastated.

Some people think that building a business that makes a lot of money is hard. While making a lot of money in a short period of time may sometimes be hard, what's really hard is making a little bit of money over a long period of time.

These three B.O.S.S. moves are the exact moves I used to scale my business to 6 and 7 figures monthly (and have also shown my clients how to do the same). Because of these three moves, I work over my business mostly, on my business some, and in my business part-time. We have 14 team members on my team (I like to think of them as team members as opposed to employees or subcontractors), and we have a payroll of tens of thousands of dollars per month, yet this business doesn't require me to be a slave to it.

I get to play golf three to six times per week. I get to spend time with my family and take world-class vacations all because of these three B.O.S.S. moves.

I don't share this with you to brag or to make you think that I am a big deal. The reason I am telling you about my personal life and the freedom that I experience from my business is to let you know that the moves that I am about to share with you are a big deal. These moves are not discriminatory. They don't care about your age, gender, or skin color. They just work.

When I used to work for other people and even when I first started my business, I would work really, really hard and make very little money. Now I work part-time a few hours per day mostly (unless we have an event), and our business sometimes generates more money in a month than I used to make in an entire decade.

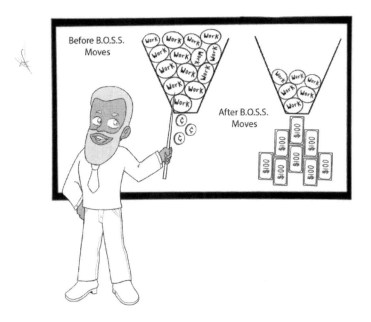

There's a reason my business and the businesses of my clients are so successful. And there are very few people in the world, if they have the willingness to do what it takes, who cannot build a business that makes them hundreds of thousands of dollars a year, or even hundreds of thousands of dollars per week.

It's even possible to build a business so successful that it could generate hundreds of thousands or millions of dollars in an hour. I know that "hundreds of thousands or millions of dollars an hour" sounds outrageous, but if you will give me just a little of your time and attention, I'll prove it to you.

I'm not going to just give you a theory.

I'm actually going to show you the framework I use to do it.

If you want to have the potential to make millions of dollars, you have to match three things. Not seven things, not 27 things. Just three things.

You need to use what I call "The B.O.S.S. Business Model," "The B.O.S.S. Business Market," and "The B.O.S.S. Message-to-Market Match."

First, you need to have the right **Business Model.** I'm going to show you the four business models. All of them work. One of them is pretty much a waste of time and energy, and the other three are legit. But in my opinion only one is a B.O.S.S. business model. So it's important to pick the right one *for you.*

Second, you must have the right **Business Market.** There are three business markets. But there is only one B.O.S.S. business market. This is one of the most important business concepts that you almost never hear discussed.

Third, you've got to have a B.O.S.S. **Message-to-Market Match.** Your message has to match the market that you're marketing to. Your message needs to be believable, desirable, and the result you promise in that message must be measurable.

If you get those three things right, your business will explode on the scene in such a way that both potential clients and competition will take notice.

The B.O.S.S. Business Model

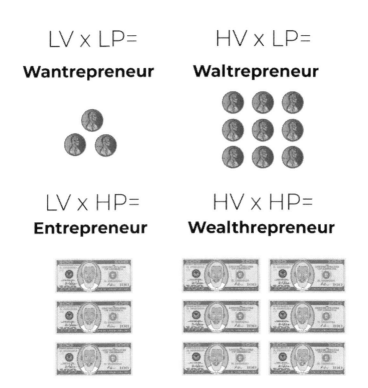

$LV \times LP =$
Wantrepreneur

$HV \times LP =$
Waltrepreneur

$LV \times HP =$
Entrepreneur

$HV \times HP =$
Wealthrepreneur

First, you must pick the right business model—for you. There's one business model that I am going to recommend you stay completely away from, but any of the other three will work. But there is one that will transform your business by giving you what I call the financial fortress formula: leverage, lifestyle, and legacy.

The first business model is the one that I do not recommend for anyone because it is the worst business model in the world. It's so bad I like to call it the business model for broke people. You can try it if you want to, but remember I warned you.

It's called: Low Volume x Low Profit, and it looks like this: LV x LP.

LV x LP = WANTrepreneurship

In the Wantrepreneur business model, you want to be a business owner, but you only know how to make low profits. And you only know how to do it at low volume. Inside Wantrepreneurship, you are not an **Entre**preneur. You are a **Want**repreneur. Don't do that anymore.

A better business model is: High Volume x Low Profit or (HV x LP).

HV x LP = WALTrepreneur.

You might be asking, what is a **Waltrepreneur?**

Well, have you ever heard of a man named Sam Walton? Or a little company called Walmart?

Sam Walton generated so much wealth from this business model that he became the richest man in the world. He was so wealthy that when he died, he was five times wealthier than Bill Gates. And then when he died and left his wealth to his wife and children, they became the second, third, fourth, fifth, and sixth wealthiest people in the world.

Sam Walton's entire business model was based on selling a lot of stuff for a little profit, and that is why it is called the Waltrepreneur business model (low profit x high volume). E-commerce is the epitome of this business model.

You can be a Waltreprenuer if you choose to. You may like e-commerce, and that's a real way to create wealth, but you need to sell a lot of volume. You've got to sell a lot of bicycle bells, a lot of pancake turners, or whatever. If you can sell 100,000 of them a day, you can get rich.

That is not my business model, but it works for some people. And I'm not going to lie to you, there are people making 6- and 7-figure incomes on Amazon with this model, but in my opinion, there is a much better way!

I don't like a business that requires me to keep up with a lot of little details. I call that minutiae, and I pay somebody to handle all of that.

Let's look at the third business model.

This is a business model that a lot of people like: Low Volume x High Profit or (LV x HP).

This is where a lot of entrepreneurs start, and this is where I got started as an entrepreneur. I'd make something that cost me $1 and sell it for much more than that.

I wrote a book called *From the Trash Man to the Cash Man: How Anyone Can Get Rich Starting From Anywhere*. If it costs me $.75 to get the book printed and I sell it for $20, how many copies would I need to sell to get rich?

We sold 150,000 copies of that book on this business model.

Let's do the math on that:

150,000 units x $.75 (cost) = $112,500

150,000 units x $20 (price) = $3,000,000

$3,000,000 (sales) - $112,500 (cost) = $2,887,500 (profit)

That's an almost $3M profit on a $20 book.

Twenty dollars is not a high price, but it's a high profit if the cost to produce each book is $.75. That puts it into the LV x HP category. Yes, I know what you're thinking. Our volume *was* pretty high, but I want you to understand that regardless of the volume, this is the world most entrepreneurs operate in.

LV x HP=
Entrepreneur

If you have a webinar that sells a $1,000 product, and you're making 10 sales per month, then you're generating $10,000 a month. That means you're making money and you are a real **Entrepreneur.**

It's not the best business model, but it's good. You can feed your babies. You can go on vacations. But it's still not my favorite business model.

Do you want to know what my favorite business model is?

This is the business model I actually use in my business. Not only is it my favorite business model but it is also the fastest and easiest path to cash. If you haven't heard me say it before …

Wealth has a need for speed.

This is the model that gives me the ability to work in my business part-time and still have plenty of time to do the things I love.

It is High Volume x High Profit or (HV x HP).

High Profit *times* High Volume? Sign me up for that program!

A lot of people find this hard to believe, and you will be hard-pressed to find a lot of people that will tell you this, but I'm going to tell you the truth.

It is much easier—it is SO much easier—to sell a high-profit, high-volume product than it is to sell a low-profit, low-volume product.

I'm going to tell you something else that I know to be true: It is exponentially easier to sell a $50,000 program than it is to sell a $5,000 program. I know that sounds backward to you, but I'm going to need you to stick with me on this one.

HV x HP=
Wealthrepreneur

If you are thinking, *Myron I'd like to believe you, but you've got to be some sort of out-of-your-mind*, then you don't understand human psychology yet. Of course, you have to be able to produce a result for people. I mean, you can't just sell something that costs $50,000 that has no value.

Later on in this book, I'm going to peel back the curtain and show you a process that you will be able to sell to anybody for $50,000 or $5,000.

Before we get to that, you have to understand human psychology. Here is the first principle of human psychology you have to understand: Human psychology tells me that if I am the cheapest, nobody will believe I'm the best.

If people believe I'm the *best*, they don't expect me to be the *cheapest. If I'm the cheapest, nobody believes I'm the best.* And when they absolutely, positively have to produce a result or die, they only want the best.

For example, if you needed a heart surgeon, could you see yourself Googling: "Cheapest heart surgeon in America"? That's not what you would put in the search! You wouldn't be calling your spouse, asking, *"Hey baby, do you know any discount heart surgeons?"* When you need a heart surgeon, you don't want the cheapest. You're going to want the best. Am I right?

So, how does all this apply to your business?

Look, if you are the cheapest, you are essentially telling everyone, "If you want the best, buy it from somebody else."

What does Walmart say? "We sell good stuff cheap." Well, I don't want cheap stuff. All I hear Walmart saying is, "We sell cheap stuff cheap." So I don't go to Walmart.

Don't get me wrong, I love Sam Walton as a businessman. I love the fact that he's created a solution for people who want cheap stuff. But I don't like cheap stuff. For example, I don't want cheap eggs. They are smaller than the best eggs and don't taste as good. If I am going to eat some eggs, I want the best eggs.

I only get to do this life one time. I only get to eat breakfast *one time* today, so I want it to be the best breakfast. I only get to eat lunch *one time* today, so I want it to be the *best* lunch. If I go on vacation one time a year, I want it to be the *best* vacation! And even if I go on vacation 10 times, they all only happen once! Do you get it? You only get each day, each moment, each experience once, so you might as well make them all the best!

Create a scenario that shows people that *you are the best.*

I'm going to tell you something. Showing people that you are the best—as hard as this is for you to wrap your mind around—begins with having a high price.

You may be asking, *But how can that be?*

Let's say, for example, that I put my Bentley Continental GT on Facebook Marketplace, and I offer to sell it for $300. What is the first question that comes to your mind?

What's wrong with it?

Right?

You see, you already understand human nature, but you think it's easier to sell your $297 product than it is to sell a $20,000 product because you don't understand that people are wondering: *What's wrong with it?*

Now, let's say you have a $10 bill. I tell you that I am going to sell you a $20 bill for $10. Would you take that deal? Does it sound like a good idea to double your money?

Alright, now that I have a $10 bill, I'm going to offer to sell it to you for $1. One dollar will get you this nice, new $10 bill.

Now, would you take that deal? Do you think it's a good idea to 10X your money?

Imagine taking me up on that offer. You just 10X'd your money. Do you even care how much you gave me? No! Who cares what the price was if you can make 10X your money, right?

I have another offer for you. Do you have a penny? Not a quarter. Not a dime. A penny.

I'm going to sell you the dollar I have for a penny.

Do you see how that's the best deal of all? If you trade me a penny for a dollar, you have just 100X'd your investment.

You've got to understand how to think from the standpoint of the marketplace. All you're thinking is, *I want to sell this stuff,* but put yourself in the shoes of the marketplace. You don't even know what their desired result is. *That's* why you don't know how to sell to them.

I don't know if you realize it, but I just taught you my pricing model. It's that simple.

When you can clearly show somebody that the payoff is twice as much, 10 times as much, or even 100 times as much as you're charging them, it doesn't matter what the price is.

When the value is as big as the state of Texas and the price is as big as a sailboat, they will buy every time.

The problem is that you think of $50,000 and say the price is too high. You're looking at the wrong metrics. It's not that the price is too high. It's that the value is too low.

What if you could show somebody how to 10X the amount of money they invested in themselves *with you*. They're not investing in you or investing in me. They are investing in themselves *through* you.

YOU are the vehicle through which your clients are investing in *themselves*.

The B.O.S.S. Business Market

If you take the right business model and put it in the right business market, it's going to be really hard for you not to get paid. When this happens, you get paid so much money you get to turn paid into a two-syllable word!

Before you can figure out the right business market for you, you have to understand what the three business markets are:

Commodity Markets (CM)

Middle Mass Markets (MMM)

Premium Markets (PM)

When most people become entrepreneurs, they fight their way to get into the worst market. It's like being the winner of the losers, like being the top of the bottom, or the best of the worst.

The first market is the commodity market. I almost can't talk about it because it makes me a little nauseous. I hate commodity markets, I don't want to sell commodities, and I don't want to be a commodity.

In a commodity market, the competition sets the price.

What does that mean?

Let's say I own a hardware store, and I sell nails for $4 per box of 100.

Sarah owns a hardware store across town, and she decides to sell her box of 100 nails for $3.90. When I realize what Sarah is selling nails for, I am forced to change my price from $4 per box to $3.80 or lose all my sales to Sarah.

It's a race to the bottom.

Before long, I hate my business. I work all day for something like 13 cents. It's a terrible business model because the competition sets the price.

Plus, zero communication happens until the person is ready to buy. A customer asks, "How much are these nails?" I say $3.80. Turns out, Sarah has hers on sale this week for $3.50, so the customer leaves and drives across town to Sarah's Hardware Store.

It's a terrible market. Why would I want to be in that?

The best way to sell is to have conversations with your customers *before* they are ready to buy.

If you're in a commodity market, no conversation happens with your customer until they come up to you and say, "How much is this?" That's a horrible way to do business. That's why I stay out of commodity markets.

The next one is middle mass markets. Cars, houses, and clothes are middle mass markets. The reason I don't like middle mass markets is because the price is set by the cost of goods.

If it costs you $100,000 to build a house, and you mark it up 30% and sell it for $130,000, you would make a 30% margin after you pay everything. Actually, you would have closer to a 15% net margin, after payroll and cost of goods are deducted.

I don't like a 15% net margin. After everything is paid, I like a 60% net margin, or a 70% margin, or even an 80% net margin.

The other thing I don't like about middle mass markets (other than the cost of goods sets the price) is that people can have conversations about your product away from you, without you even being there, and then come and tell you how much they're willing to pay you for your stuff.

They say, "I looked it up on Zillow. This house is only worth $102,000 and you want $130,000?" And then they say, "I'll go buy from somebody else."

That's not how I work. This is how I do it … I say, "This is mine and I'm selling, so you're going to pay me what I'm telling you you're going to pay."

I hate middle mass markets. I don't want to sell a car. I don't want to sell a house. I don't want to sell something where I can only make a 30% gross margin and a 15% net margin. That is awful. Well, it's not *awful*. There are people who have become millionaires and billionaires on that model, but they could have become a trillionaire if they'd listened to me, right? Well, potentially.

The last business market is my favorite, and in my opinion, the best. This is where I sing and dance. This is where I play, where I hang out. It's where all my people are. This is where I get paid. It's the sweet spot. It's called premium value markets.

What does premium mean? Premium means expensive. High price. And I like to add high value!

The reason you think it's hard to sell a high-ticket offer is because you're selling to broke people. You're selling to cheap-ple people and free-ple people and you need to find some pre-ple people.

They are called cheap-ple people and free-ple because they are people who want stuff for cheap or for free. Pre-ple people want premium goods so they're willing to pay a premium price.

The B.O.S.S. Message-to-Market Match

If your message appeals to everyone, your message appeals to no one.

You've got to have the right message-to-market match.

You have to create a message that is specifically for the people who you desire to sell your premium value products to. When you do that, it's going to repel all the free-ple people, all the cheap-ple people, and the only people left when the dust settles will be the pre-ple people—the people who are willing to pay a premium for the value you are offering them.

Make sure your messaging attracts the people who value the result you can produce and drives everybody else away who will waste your time.

I don't have my lowest price main offer as a $55,430 offer because I want everybody. Let me be honest with you, I want people who are struggling to make ends meet to know I am not their dude.

Listen, if you are struggling to make ends meet, buy my book *From the Trash Man to the Cash Man: How Anyone Can Get Rich Starting from Anywhere* because you're just not ready to work with me yet.

Here is what you need to do: You need to figure out the payoff that you can produce.

Ok, now I'm going to peel back the curtain and show you all the fruit-juicy secrets on how you can go to Your Town, USA, or wherever you live in the world, and build a business that does $100,000 a month … or if you can't process that big yet, $20,000 a month, or whatever your dream number is.

I'm going to show you how to do that, but first you've got to learn how to get out of your own mind and out of your own way!

Let me ask you a question.

Have you noticed that when I talk about large sums of money, or what most people think of as large sums of money, I talk about them like they're not that big of a deal?

For me, $100,000 a month is nice, but if I only made $100,000 a month, I'd be like, "What'd I do wrong? Where'd I mess up? I mean, I know I've played golf every day, but it wasn't that bad, was it?"

I'm keeping it real. Broke people think I'm doing that to show off, but that's not it at all! I don't need you to think anything about me at all. I don't need you to be impressed with me.

The reason I talk about $100,000 a month like it's not a big thing is for myself. I do it for me, not you. You just get to hear how I talk to myself.

You see, one of the things that I discovered on the path to creating wealth is that you never make more than the amount you allow yourself to think of as a lot of money.

Do you remember how much money you made when you got your first job? Was it three dollars an hour? Five dollars an hour? Ten dollars an hour?

The first job I had was when I was 14 years old and it paid $1.55 an hour.

Are you willing to work for $3 an hour now? Are you willing to work for $10 an hour now? I certainly am not willing to work for $1.55 an hour.

We all have an amount that we're not willing to work for, right? We have a number that if somebody says, "I'll pay you $15 an hour," we think, *Well, you might pay somebody that looks like me $15 an hour, but it ain't gonna be me.*

Am I telling the truth?

The key difference is that I raised my point to a higher number. If you want to work with me one-on-one right now, it's going to cost you $25,000 an hour. And that's real talk. If too many people take me up on it, it's going to be even more than that.

Why? Because I can go and talk for 90 minutes and I can make $180,000. I don't want to be spending all day coaching people for $25,000 an hour. It's not worth my time.

I will do like an hour or two a week maybe, but I really don't even like to do that. Now, you might not like that I charge so much for one-on-one coaching. What I am saying right now might even make you uncomfortable.

And here is the thing, if you have a problem with who I am, I want to challenge you on that. Your real problem is who you think *you* are; and worse, who you think you're *not*.

It's not my fault you haven't raised your prices and are not selling what you are worth.

Remember, you will never make more than the amount you allow yourself to think of as a lot of money. I don't allow myself to think of $1 million as a lot of money, so it's easy for me to have a million-dollar offer.

If someone asks how much I charge for this offer, I say, "It's $1 million, and I'm going to help you make $10 million in the next 12 months. I am going to map out exactly how we're going to do it."

Keep in mind, though, that in order to sell a million-dollar offer, you need to have a million-dollar offer.

Who's going to buy an offer like that?

Business owners who see the value in your offer.

You must understand how to create value.

Here are the next questions you must ask yourself:

> Is your business going to be B2C (B-to-C), Business to Consumer?
>
> Is it going to be B2B (B-to-B), Business to Business?
>
> Or is it going to be B2G (B-to-G), Business to Government?

Right now, I have very little B2C stuff. Very little. I only sell a couple of books and a little membership site for consumers. Most of the stuff I do is B2B.

I'm going to move into B2G, where I go into a government and help them revitalize their entire economy, and have them pay me hundreds of millions of dollars to help them reevaluate.

Here is what you have to understand: The principles are what do the work. All principles always work the same for everybody. Principles don't care how tall you are, how short you are, how young you are, how old you are, what color you are, what gender you are. Principles don't care, they just work.

When you apply the principles, they work for you just like they worked for Russell Brunson, just like they worked for Myron Golden, just like they worked for all the business gurus.

What you have to figure out is, "What value can I offer a business owner right now?"

Here is what you need to know: You've got to have the right business model, the right business market, and the right business message. Then, you've got to go to business owners and show those business owners how to grow their businesses.

You want to be able to go in and show them how to dominate the marketplace and crush the competition.

How do you do that?

I'm going to tell you a little secret.

Are you ready for this?

There are only four ways to grow a business.

That's right. Only four.

GROW YOUR BUSINESS
LIKE A B.O.S.S.

In the next few pages, I am going to show you how to grow your business like a B.O.S.S.—a Business Optimization Success Strategist. You'll discover how to scale a business from $10,000 per month to $128,000 per month in only four moves. And if you add zeros to those numbers, the formula still applies.

Do you think you can remember four moves?

Before I tell you what those moves are, I want you to know something.

Every business growth coach and consultant all teach the same four moves. Russell Brunson teaches the same four moves I do, and I teach the same four moves he does. We teach the same four moves Frank Kern does, and he teaches the same four moves Tony Robbins does. That's because when it comes to growing and scaling businesses, there are only four moves.

If you have a business that you would like to scale, then you must make these four moves. When you figure out how to effectively activate these hyper-growth business strategies, your business will grow exponentially.

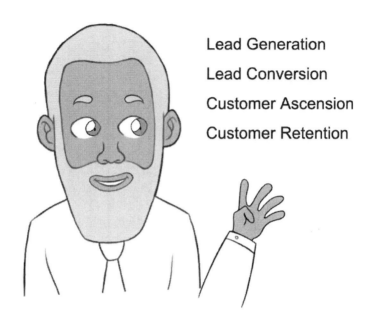

Lead Generation

Lead Conversion

Customer Ascension

Customer Retention

Are you ready for the four B.O.S.S. Moves? They are:

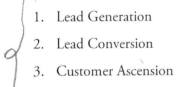

1. Lead Generation

2. Lead Conversion

3. Customer Ascension

4. Customer Retention

Let's take them one at a time, then put them together, and watch what happens next.

To keep the math simple, we'll use small, even numbers. Keep in mind, though, that it doesn't matter what the numbers are. The principles still apply.

First, you need to look at what actions you're taking to consistently hit your monthly revenue number. Next, you need to find out what you're doing that's keeping you stuck at that number.

Let's assume you have a core product offer (CPO) of $1,000, so every time you make a sale, you're making $1,000. If your business is doing $10,000 per month in revenue, that means you're generating 10 sales per month.

In order to generate those sales, you first have to generate leads, right? So, let's say you're generating 100 leads per month. And let's assume you have a 10% conversion rate. Since 10% of 100 is 10, that gets you 10 sales per month. Get the picture? Good.

Now, let's scale your business by more than 10X. How do we do that using only four moves?

B.O.S.S. Move #1: Lead Generation

The first move you need to make is to increase the number of leads you generate. If you double your number of leads from 100 to 200, and everything else stays the same, then you just doubled your business revenue and profit.

You only did one of the four B.O.S.S. Moves, and you already doubled your business. In other words, you fixed one thing but you're making twice as much. Instead of making $10,000 per month, you're now making $20,000 per month.

Double your revenue by doubling your leads.

Now, you're probably thinking to yourself, *That sounds great, Myron, but how do I do that?*

Have you ever heard of an opt-in funnel? How about a lead capture page? If you have a business and you are not currently using an opt-in funnel or lead capture page, adding this one component to your business could potentially lead to mind-blowing growth.

Do you know how many millions of businesses in the United States of America and abroad have never heard of an opt-in funnel? If you are a business growth coach or consultant, you could make a fortune just by teaching business owners how to capture leads.

In fact, you could build an opt-in funnel for business owners and have them pay you for the leads. After the business owner gets the leads, it's up to them to convert those leads into paying customers.

This is not hard stuff.

Now, this is where the magic starts to happen.

B.O.S.S. Move #2: Lead Conversion

The next thing you do to grow your business is to improve your lead conversion process. You improve your lead conversions by improving your sales process.

The sales process that I teach will enable you to work with human nature instead of working against it. When you work with human nature, it works for you. When you work against human nature, it works against you—which, by the way, is a battle you can't win.

Let's start with what I call Psychological Artistry. This is the art of painting word pictures and hanging them in the minds of your prospect to help them see the world in a whole new light. You'll see lots of examples of this throughout this book if you're looking for them.

Along with Psychological Artistry, my sales framework relies heavily on Emotional Cooperation and Logical Justification.

When you use Emotional Cooperation in selling, you are creating an environment that makes your prospects feel like buying. With Logical Justification, you're supporting that feeling with logical reasons to buy.

You've got to make your prospects feel like buying.

Again, you might be thinking, *Myron, that sounds great, but how do I do that?* Good question.

You can reach Emotional Cooperation by using what Russell Brunson calls "The Big Domino and Three Secrets."

31

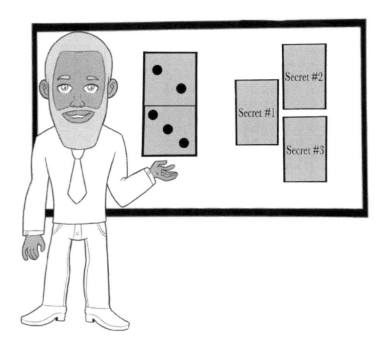

The Big Domino is the main thing you have to get people to believe in order to say yes to your offer. The Three Secrets are what Russell uses to break old beliefs that would stop them from taking on the new belief, causing them to say yes to your offer. In a nutshell, the Three Secrets are:

- Change their primary limiting belief about your offer.

- Change their external limiting belief about your offer.

- Change their internal limiting belief about your offer.

Most people don't know about the Big Domino and Three Secrets. And I'm not going to go into detail about it in this book, but it's all laid out in Russell Brunson's *Expert Secrets* book. So if you haven't already read *Expert Secrets*, go buy it, read it, and do what it says.

If you use any of the above-mentioned frameworks to convert more sales, you could easily double your conversion rates. If you go from a 10% conversion rate to a 20% conversion rate, you've just doubled your revenue again!

Think about it—you doubled your lead generation from 100 leads per month to 200 leads per month. Then, you doubled your conversions from 10% to 20%. Since 20% of 200 is 40, you are now making 40 sales per month with your $1,000 core product.

Wait a minute. Did you see what just happened?

We only made two moves. First we doubled your leads (100 to 200), then we doubled your conversions (10% to 20%). And that's assuming your leads stayed the same as you were improving your conversions.

If you were at $10,000 a month with a $1,000 core offer, you scaled to $20,000 a month with the first move and to $40,000 with the next move. You quadrupled your business by doing only two of the four B.O.S.S. Moves for exponentially growing and scaling a business!

B.O.S.S. Move #3: Customer Ascension

The third move isn't about leads. It's about customers and clients. That's because once you generate leads and convert them into buyers, those prospects are no longer leads. They're customers. They've converted (or transformed) into your client base. Now it's time to ascend them.

Customer ascension simply means you are going to add a "Premium Value Offer" to your mix. Most people who understand this concept call it a "High Ticket Offer." I like to describe it based on what the client gets from the encounter more than what I get. That's why I use the term Premium Value Offer (PVO) instead of High Ticket Offer (HTO).

Let's say you create a $10,000 PVO and you offer it to all of the people who bought your $1,000 CPO. Let's also say for the sake of this illustration that you convert 10% of those buyers to also take advantage of your PVO.

Since 10% of 40 sales per month is four, and four times $10,000 is $40,000, you just added an extra $40,000 per month to your revenue. This is probably my favorite B.O.S.S. Move. If you add this $40,000 to the $40,000 per month from your increased leads and conversions, you are now at $80,000 per month.

If you don't already have a PVO, then pay special attention to this next section. You need to understand something most people get backward.

One of the most important things that I ever do for my clients—one of the most valuable things that I do for them—is charge them a premium to work with me.

You might wonder: *Myron, don't you do that for yourself?*

No, because I don't need their money. But they need to pay me.

Why?

Because you sell like you buy. People who are unwilling to pay will be unable to charge. If you desire to sell premium value offers, you must be a buyer of premium value offers. It's a right of passage.

People who want to sell premium value offers—but who have never bought a premium value offer—are not only deceiving themselves but they are also deceiving their prospects. They think they will be able to help someone cross over to the world of PVOs, but they, themselves, have never crossed over. They don't even really believe in the process.

You sell like you buy.

When I sell somebody a PVO, I am freeing them to sell somebody else a PVO because now they know people are willing to pay $20,000 or $50,000 or $80,000, even $100,000.

Why?

Because *they* just did.

If you buy a $50,000 program, you're not going to have a hard time charging somebody $10,000.

The limitations that you have are in your mind.

All you need to say is, "This is how much it is to work with me. I charge $10,000. Do you want to pay that up front or in two or three payments?"

You do that for 10 businesses per month, and you will make over a million dollars in a year on one offer.

When you stop putting more faith in your limitations than you do in your leverage, you will begin to experience a life of flow.

I'm going to tell you what I know for a fact to be true. You don't have to take my word for it. I would recommend that you do your own research, but I know beyond any shadow of doubt that the master key to success in any achievement is to *take ownership of the result before you know the path.*

Stop thinking, "As soon as I know how to do it, I'm going to do it."

Start thinking, "I'm going to do it and figure it out while I'm doing it."

Don't say, "I'll do it as soon as I learn how." Because you don't even get to start learning how until you start doing it.

The master key to wealth—to having a quantum leap—is to start to leap before you know how you're going to land.

Take ownership of the result before you know the path.

At this point, we've done only three of the four moves to grow a business. We've doubled the number of leads and doubled the number of conversions. For the buyers of the CPO, we've added a PVO with a 10% conversion rate.

That means we've taken your business from $10,000 a month to $80,000 a month. That's $960,000 per year, and you haven't even made the last move yet!

What's the last move?

B.O.S.S. Move #4: Customer Retention

You've got to improve your retention. But how do you do that?

You improve retention through continuity.

Continuity means you sell the product once but get paid for it every year, or every month or every week. There are several kinds of products that work well for continuity: newsletters, SAAS (software as a service), memberships, etc.

One of my favorite continuity models is a Forced Continuity Offer or FCO. Let's say, for example, that you sell a course or coaching program teaching someone to do something that they already want to learn how to do, but you teach them how to do it by using software that makes that task easier.

You give them a free 30-day or 90-day trial of the software. Then, once they understand the value of it and are used to using it, you start charging for the use of the software.

For easy math, let's say you add a $100 per month SAAS offer to your $1,000 CPO. You could even make it mandatory. If someone wants to purchase your CPO, they'll also need to purchase your SAAS offer (ideally, after a free trial).

At 40 sales per month, that's a total of 480 sales at the end of a year. If you multiply those 480 sales times the forced continuity purchase for $100 per month, that's $48,000 per month.

When you add the $48,000 per month from the FCO to the $40,000 per month from the PVO added to the $40,000 per month from the CPO, that's a total of $128,000 per month in four B.O.S.S. Moves.

You see how easy that was?

When you make your offer, you have to keep in mind that you are not the result, and you don't produce the results for your clients. You sell the outcome, and the process produces the result.

Now, you might be asking yourself, *Myron, how do I sell the outcome?*

Well, I'm glad you asked. My presentation is simple. I say:

> "If I can show you how to take a business that's making $10,000 a month and tweak four things (not 57 things, not 77 things) ... We'll tweak four things, and your business is going to go from making $10,000 a month in revenue to doing $128,000 per month in revenue (potentially) ... When I can show you the math ... would you be happy with me? Would you want me to keep working with you? Or would you rather I go work with your competitor?"

You can argue with a lot of things and win, but math ain't one of them. So show them the math. If they don't buy, they're dumb as a box of rocks, and they're not going to pay you anyway.

Is that too basic?

Nothing I shared with you is theory. Everything I shared with you is exactly what I do. I just peeled back the curtain and showed you what the magician knows so it doesn't have to be magic to you anymore.

THE B.O.S.S.
LEVELS OF VALUE

If you want to create wealth, you need to understand the four levels of value, and you need to understand that how much money you generate will directly correlate to which level you are operating in. If you desire to create the most wealth you must operate at the highest level.

You cannot expect to create more value at a lower level and generate the same amount of income as someone operating at the highest level. Instead, you need to figure out how to operate at a higher level of value. Then you can offer less, and still make way more money.

Before we get to what the four levels of value are, you first need to understand something that most people haven't even thought about, much less understand, and that is this:

Money is spiritual.

What do I mean by that? Money is not material in its essence. Money is instead spiritual in nature.

People say, *I don't want to be rich; I'm not that materialistic.* Well, which is it? You don't want to be rich or you're not that materialistic? Because remember, money is not material in its essence any more than human beings are material in their essence.

Physical money is simply a representation of a particular value. It looks material, but its essence is spiritual. It can go anywhere; it flows through space and time.

Let me explain further. If I have a penny and a $100 bill, which one is worth more? The penny or the $100 bill?

Some say the penny is worth more because the material the penny is made out of (metal) is worth more than the material the $100 bill is made out of (paper/cotton), yet, the $100 bill is worth 10,000 times more than the penny.

How is this possible? Because the value of money is not based on the material it's made of.

So what is the value of money?

The value of money is based on the message it carries (in other words, "language"), and language is spiritual. You see, only spiritual beings have language. We can tell how much a unit of money is worth based on what's written on it. If it says "one-cent" then the money is worth 1/100 of a dollar. If the unit of money says "$100," then it is worth 10,000 times the value of a penny.

The other thing that makes money valuable is the fact that we believe it's valuable. You see, there is nothing backing the money of most countries. The only thing backing it is the fact that the people of the country believe it has value. So the value of money is based on the message it carries and the faith that it creates.

Language and faith are both spiritual attributes, not materialistic ones. So the value of money is not based on anything materialistic.

We can take it even further by saying that only spiritual things can be in more than one place at a time. Think about it, you can have money in your bank account, a checkbook for that account in your desk drawer, and a debit card for that account, and they all represent the exact same money.

How can that money be in three places at once? Because money is spiritual.

If you desire to increase the amount of money that you earn, you must learn to operate on a higher spiritual level.

Now that you understand that money, communication, and imagination are all spiritual, let's dive into the Four Levels of Value.

Imagination

Communication

Unification

Implementation

Implementation: Level 1

The lowest level of value in the marketplace is **Implementation.**

The person who "does the thing" makes the least amount of money.

For example, in a hotel, the hardest working people in the hotel are the housekeeping staff, but why do they make the least amount of money? They make the least amount of money because they are the people who *do the thing*.

The resources people use to make money on this level are time and their muscles. Muscles are a physical resource, and time is a limited resource. This is why it's so hard to create wealth on this level. You are attempting to use physical and limited resources to produce an unlimited spiritual result.

The reason that God set it up that way, (yes, that's what I said, God set it up that way) is because money is a spiritual result.

If you're using a physical resource to produce a spiritual result, the spiritual result has to be limited because physical resources are limited. You want to use spiritual resources to create spiritual results because spiritual resources are not limited.

Unification: Level 2

The next level of value is **Unification.**

On the implementation level, you are using your muscles to make money. On the unification level, you use your management skills to make money.

These are the people who manage the people who do the things.

Managing the people who are doing the thing is a higher spiritual task than just doing the thing yourself. That's why managers make more money than the people they manage.

You can make maybe $250,000 a year in the unification level if you're a manager of Lockheed Martin or Boeing or Southwest, or one of those other Fortune 500 companies.

However, what many people don't understand is you can't expect to get rich on the lower levels of value.

If you want to start creating wealth, you have to operate in the two highest levels.

Communication: Level 3

The second-highest level of value is **Communication.**

Remember that language is spiritual—it is something only spiritual beings have. That's why the person who writes the book makes more money than the person who prints the book.

Understand that if you really want to get good at making money, you've got to get good at using your mouth to create messages that move the masses. Get good at using your mouth to have conversations that create cash flow.

I can make way more money talking than you can make with every muscle in your body.

Wealth begins on the communication level.

It doesn't matter if you're an author, if you're a speaker, if you're a salesperson, if you're an actor, if you're a singer, if you're a songwriter, if you're a playwright … all of those people are communicating.

They communicate a message to the masses, and they have the potential to make millions.

Imagination: Level 4

The highest level of value is **Imagination**.

The people who come up with the best ideas are the ones who create the most wealth.

I'm going to name a company, and I want you to name the first person that comes to your mind:

Apple Corporation.

Everybody says Steve Jobs, even though he died eight years ago and hasn't invented anything since then. Besides that, he didn't even invent the Apple computer, Steve Wozniak did. But when you say Apple, people don't say Tim Cook or Steve Wozniak.

Why? Because Steve Wozniak was the implementer who made the Apple products. Steve Jobs was the *imagineer* that made Apple what it was.

The people who come up with the best ideas are the ones who change the world.

Thinking is a higher spiritual activity than speaking. So, if you want to make more money, *think* and grow rich.

Think at a higher level. Speak, communicate, and grow rich at a higher level.

THE B.O.S.S. SKILL
YOU MUST MASTER

I f you want to make a lot of money, if you want to change a lot of lives, you've got to get good at selling.

Selling is not talking people into buying things they don't want, don't need, and can't afford.

Selling is uncovering the value of what you have to offer so well that people are happy to exchange the money they have in their pockets for the value you've revealed.

What It Means to Uncover Value

The problem is, when we think about uncovering value to people, we think about uncovering what's valuable to us about our thing.

That's not the same thing as uncovering value to people. Because guess what, they don't care about your thing. And don't worry, it's not just you.

They don't care about my thing either.

They don't like you that much.

They don't like me that much.

I'm just keeping it real.

They like themselves, period.

So nobody's going to listen to you talk to them about your stuff … because they don't care.

Before you can offer something of value to someone, you have to uncover what's valuable to that someone.

In order to uncover the value of what's valuable to that someone, you have to ask questions and wait for an answer. Or you at least have to pay attention to what people are complaining about.

People only pay you for solving their problems. They're not going to pay you for solving the problems you want to solve.

You might be thinking, *Yeah, but I've always wanted to do this!* That's nice. Make it a hobby. It doesn't deserve to be your business.

You want to solve problems that people know they have. The bigger the problem is to the person you're solving it for, the bigger the amount of money that they will pay you for solving that problem. Does that make sense?

Good. Now, let's talk about persuasion.

Persuading Is Not Convincing

The reason people have to attempt to convince people to buy whatever it is they're selling is that they did not do a good job persuading them.

Selling is not all about making a purchase.

In fact, there's a difference between convincing and persuading.

Convincing is trying to get you to buy my thing.

If I'm convincing you, I'm trying to get you to do something I desire you to do for my reasons. You don't like me that much.

I mean, you may like me. But not that much.

Persuasion, on the other hand, is helping people make a decision they already desire to make for their own reasons.

That's why, if you want to be really, really good at sales, you have to be good at listening.

The Gift of Gab Does Not Help You Sell

You may have heard that "the gift of gab" will help you sell. The gift of gab does not help you sell. The gift of listening helps you sell.

When you get good at selling, it's because you got good at listening. Being able to talk well only helps you in selling when you are talking about the things that your prospect cares about.

Treat people like they are smart, and they will believe you are smart. Treat people with respect, and they will treat you with respect. Sell from a place of love for the client (by love, I mean you have their best interest in mind and you will only sell them something that will serve them at the highest level) and the clients will love to buy from you.

I call this allowing the client or prospect to provide the content and you provide the context. By content, I am talking about "the reasons they desire the transformation" that your solution (product, service, or program) provides. By context, I am talking about the things you draw attention to in your presentation that show the client that your solution is their best chance to achieve their transformation.

Let the client or prospect provide the content for the sale and you provide the context.

Far too many salespeople believe that talking about their product, process, program, pieces, or person will cause their prospect to buy. I've got news for you: They don't care about you or your stuff.

Don't feel bad! They don't care about me or my stuff either. They care about themselves and their stuff. When you can show them that you care about them and their stuff so much that you've actually thought about their problem more than they have, and because of this you've devised an elegant solution, then and only then will they buy from you without resistance—regardless of price.

Just remember, they provide the content for the sale and you provide the context! The content is all the facts about their desires,

the content is the frame that causes them to focus on your
~~solution~~.

Content is the solution or transformation they seek.

Context is the frame that you put around it.

It's the thing you caused them to focus on that helps them
understand why the thing you are selling them is the bridge to get
them to the destination they desire to get to.

Does that make sense? If not, go back and read that again.

If you're talking to people about an offer, and they're not taking
you up on it, they're not taking you up on it because you're
talking to them about you and your stuff. Stop talking about you.
And start talking to them about them and their stuff!

If you're saying, "You're going to get so many hours of my
time …"

Stop it.

You don't want my time, and even at $25,000 an hour, I don't
want to sell you my time. You know why? Because I can make a
whole lot more than $25,000 in an hour.

Why would I want to take a whole hour and talk to one person
for $25,000? If somebody buys too many hours, I'm raising the
price again because selling my time is highly inefficient.

Selling an hour of time to one person is inefficient.

Besides, I'm not that person's answer.

The payoff is the answer they are looking for and the process is the way to the payoff. But you don't sell them the process, you sell them the payoff and then deliver the process.

If I attempt to sell you by showing you my process, the conclusion you're going to come to on a conscious or subconscious level is: This is too hard.

So you're not going to buy it.

I never sell the process.

People don't get to learn my process until after they buy.

Don't Sell the Process, Sell the Payoff

Want to make a lot of sales?

Sell the payoff.

And when you're selling the payoff, use the word "potentially." Say to them, "You could make a lot of money, potentially." Or, "You could lose 30 lbs, potentially." Or, "You could have more energy, potentially." You are not saying "potentially" to create doubt, you are saying it to create trust and demonstrate that you are an honest person. (You are also protecting yourself against "bogus claims.")

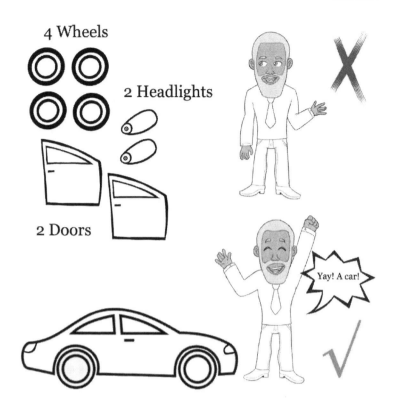

4 Wheels

2 Headlights

2 Doors

Yay! A car!

Don't sell the pieces of your offer. Don't say, "It's got one of these, and two of those, and three in green, and one in blue."

People don't care about the pieces! That's not what people want to buy. People want the payoff. They want an easy button. They want to believe it's easy even though they know work is involved. They want to know that it works. And they want to know that they can do it! Clearly show them these things in your offer and they will buy.

Now that we understand why people buy, let's talk about offers and the value ladder. I sell mostly what are known as "High Ticket" (which I like to think of as "high-value" products and services. This is my playground, and this is the arena in which I am one of the best in the world, both in selling these types of offers and teaching others how to do the same.

The lower-priced products that I sell have one purpose only: to help get people to the point that they can afford to buy my premium offers.

I've got three main offers, which are all premium offers. And I am going to recommend to you that if you don't have some premium offers yet, get some as soon as possible.

One of my offers is $81,000. That's the little one.

One of them is $155,000.

My big premium offer is $1,000,000 per year.

Here's what I know: The main reason you've never sold an $81K offer, or a $155K offer, or a $1 million offer is that you don't have one to sell.

Is that the only reason?

Maybe not the only reason, but definitely the main reason.

Do you know why you don't have one to sell?

Because you've never thought about the problem of a premium buyer more than they have to the point where you understand it at the highest level and can explain to them in a persuasive manner why your solution is their best chance to get the payoff they desire.

You've never crafted a message that shows your ideal client that your solution is worth so much more than the money that they are about to pay you that they pay you and thank you in tears for giving them the opportunity to buy!

When I'm creating an offer, the first question I ask myself is, *How much money do I want to make when I sell it?* Not: *How much money do I think I can make?*

How much money do I want to make for this thing?

That's the first question I ask myself.

Let's say the answer is $81,000.

My second question is, "How can I produce an $810,000 result for someone, 10X their investment, and make it so apparent that it is their best chance to get the outcome they've been seeking that they are happy to pay me regardless of price?"

And by the way, that is not going to come to me in five minutes.

If it takes me five days or five weeks to figure out how to produce an $810,000 result, is it worth it? There are very few things you will do in your life that are more valuable.

Your problem is that you want to run to the marketplace with an underdeveloped offer for an undervalued price, and then get mad at the world because you're struggling.

Don't do that anymore.

Take the time on the front end to make your offer valuable when you present it in the marketplace.

I like premium value markets because I set the price. If for no other reason, that's enough. *I set the price.*

If I'm going to have a business, and I'm the one doing the work in the business, doesn't it make sense that I should be the one who sets the price? I mean, am I missing something?

I set the price because I'm the one who has to do the work. I'm the one who's going to produce the result, so maybe, just maybe, I should set the price.

That's one reason I like premium value markets. Another reason I like premium value markets is that all of the conversations happen before the customer buys, and it all happens with me—and only me—in a vacuum. Because of that, I get to reveal the value *before* I reveal the price.

They know how valuable it is long before they know what the price is.

When I do a live event and I make my $81,000 offer, they have to accept the offer before they know what the price is, before they know what the pieces are, before they know what the process is.

How's that possible?

It's possible because I take a day and a half of my life to reveal to them the payoff.

They don't know what the price is. They don't know what the pieces are. The one thing they do know is the payoff.

They already know it's not cheap because I already told them that. They know it's going to be less than a house, but more than a car, because I told them.

And they say yes.

In fact, I have the people who say yes join me in the front of the room and I have everybody else clap for them. And they still don't know what they said yes to or how much it costs. They only know the payoff. But they are excited to say yes to the payoff.

Do you know what I have everybody else in the room do who did not say yes?

Leave the room. Go to lunch.

The people who do not take the offer don't even get to find out what the offer is!

I'm telling you, that is how the conversation happens in a vacuum before they know the price.

That's how you sell premium value markets, but you have to be willing to do it in that order. And when you do that, you create premium value.

I create my own premium value market.

What else do I do to create premium value?

I do community service work. That does not mean that I go around and pick up trash in the neighborhood. It means I have a podcast. I've got Facebook Lives. I've got Facebook groups. I've got YouTube channels.

I put out free content, and if I do say so myself, my free content is better than a lot of other people's paid content.

When some people put out free content, they want to put out free junk and then people never get a chance to experience the good stuff that they have for sale.

I give fruit juicy nuggets for free and they say, "If he taught me this much for free, how much will he teach me if I pay him?"

Bottom line: Figure out what your offer is and make that offer.

Everything is about an offer.

By the way, an offer is not your product. An offer is not the stack. An offer is not the pieces. An offer is the payoff. *That* is what your offer is.

What is the result they're seeking that you can get for them? That's the offer.

Until you know what that is, it doesn't matter what else you talk to them about.

You can have your free sequence ... and your big domino ... and your stack ... and everything else ... *but* ... if you don't know what the payoff is, then you have no offer.

Does that make sense?

I'm going to show you some frameworks for making offers that I have used to make millions of dollars. And it could work for you—potentially.

You see, making a lot of money is not hard. It's actually quite simple.

My business generates 6 and 7 figures a month, and I work part-time. So I know making a lot of money is not the hard part.

The hard part is becoming the person who can do the thing that makes you a lot of money, but don't worry ... we'll get to that part.

For now, I want you to remember that the first thing you should do when you get started in a business is to begin at the end and work your way backward.

What does that mean?

Figure out a high-value result you can create for a business owner, and start with a high-ticket offer.

That's the best business advice I can give anyone.

Start with a high-ticket offer.

You might be thinking: *I'm going to work my way up to a high-ticket offer. I'm going to sell a $97 thing, then a $297 thing, and then a $697 thing ...*

My advice is to figure out a high-value result you can produce for somebody and go charge them the money, and don't be scared.

Now you might be thinking, *What if they say no?*

I'm going to let you in on a little secret.

If you don't make the offer, then it's already a no.

Since I already got a no, I can either keep the no, or I can give myself a chance to get a yes.

Are you picking up what I'm putting down?

Just remember this ...

An offer you don't make
is an offer they can't take.

Alright, now it's time to learn what it really means to learn, how to learn the right way, and how to do it fast—because the faster you learn, the faster you earn.

SECTION II

Speed Learning
Like a B.O.S.S.

THE FASTER YOU LEARN, THE MORE YOU EARN

H ave you ever felt overwhelmed by all of the stuff you have to learn?

The world changes so fast that sometimes it makes you feel like you can't keep up, but I've got good news for you: You *can* keep up.

You can absolutely keep up with all the things you have to learn, but you have to learn in a specific way. And it's not the way that you've been taught to learn all your life. It's not about memorizing a bunch of right answers and then being able to spout off those right answers at the right time.

That's not actually how learning takes place.

I'm going to share with you some strategies on how you can take your level of learning in any arena to the next level—and then the next level—until you get to the level of total mastery.

The Levels of Competency

People talk about the fact that when you first get started in something, you are an "unconscious incompetent." That is, you don't know, and you don't even know why you don't know.

And then you go from being an unconscious incompetent to being a "conscious incompetent." That means you don't know, but at least you're aware of the fact that you don't know.

And then you become an "unconscious competent." You are doing what works, but you don't know why it works.

And then you become a "conscious competent." That means that you are doing what works and you know why it works, so you can go and do it again.

That works as a mental model, a way of representing what learning really is—how learning actually takes place … but I'm going to help you take it to another level.

When I was growing up, I was a Bruce Lee fan. And I guess I still am because I was filling out one of those bank secret questions—you know how they ask you a secret question to verify your identification? Well, it asked me, "Who's your favorite celebrity?"

And the only person I could think of was Bruce Lee.

Bruce Lee made a lot of movies. He made *Enter the Dragon* and *Return of the Dragon* and *The Chinese Connection* and *The Big Boss*. Then, he died while he was working on his last movie. Ironically, it's called *The Game of Death*.

Basically, he had to go into this tower and he had to fight all these guys. And if he beat the guy on level one, then he got to go up to the next level.

It was kind of like a game.

He got to go up to the next level and beat the guy on level two, and then got to go to the next level.

If he beat the guy on level three, he got to go up to the next level, and he just kept on going until he got to the top of the tower.

Well, that analogy is a good analogy for us to use for the idea of learning.

From this day forward, I don't want you to think of learning information as accumulating a bunch of stuff that you know.

I want you to think of it more like a game with levels.

Think of learning as a game with levels.

What Is Learning?

Before we talk about the levels of learning, let's take a minute to talk about wisdom. You will come to understand that wisdom has a lot to do with learning.

But to start, wisdom has some prerequisites:

Wisdom Prerequisite #1: Ignorance

Ignorance is the absence of truth.

Wisdom Prerequisite #2: Knowledge

Knowledge is the accumulation of truth.

Wisdom Prerequisite #3: Understanding

Understanding is the assimilation of truth.

And then, lastly, you get to wisdom.

Wisdom is the application of truth.

Wisdom is not just knowing what to do, but it's knowing how to do it—*and then actually doing what you know.*

From now on, when you think of learning, I want you to think of learning as a synonym for wisdom, instead of thinking of learning as a synonym for IQ or intelligence.

Learning is a synonym for wisdom.

Unfortunately, most people equate learning with knowledge, and knowledge is certainly a part of learning, but they believe that accumulating a bunch of knowledge about a thing is learning. But is knowing about something really learning?

Knowledge about a thing is part of learning, but it's not wisdom.

I want to change your definition of learning so you can use it as a synonym for wisdom.

In other words, I am learning *about* a thing, so I can learn *to do* the thing, so I can then *do the thing.*

Let me say that again.

I want you to think of learning as gaining wisdom by learning *about* a thing so that you can learn *to do* the thing so that you can then *do the thing.*

See, we grew up believing—buying into the lie—that learning about something is the same as learning that thing, but it's not.

You already know that it's not.

All of us have read books and then after we got done reading the book, we were not able to implement the things that were in the book.

All of us have gone to a seminar, and after the seminar, we did not implement the things that we were taught in the seminar.

All of us have gone to church and heard a sermon and then did not implement the things that were in the sermon.

So, we know intuitively that learning about something is not actually learning. If you've accumulated a bunch of facts around the thing, you haven't really learned anything.

We know that intuitively, but somehow or another, we don't allow ourselves to accept that knowing about something is not enough. I believe we keep coming back to knowing about things instead of really learning things because we don't have a mental model of what learning really is.

Let me give you a mental model for what learning really is: Learning is learning *about* a thing so you can learn *to do* a thing, so you can then go *do the thing*.

If you don't ever get to the place where you can *do the thing*, then you did not learn the thing.

You may have learned *about* it, but *you didn't learn it.*

Hopefully, that's resonating with you and you're getting it.

I don't want you to feel bad about the things that you've learned *about* but have not learned to *do*. The reason I'm sharing this information with you is so that you won't, in the future, make the mistake of thinking that knowing *about* something or learning *about* something is the same as *learning* it.

I don't want you to be satisfied when you learn some information about a subject but you still have no ability to implement it.

I want you to keep on leveling up until you get to the place where not only do you know how to do the thing, but you are *doing* the thing, and you are doing it *competently*.

I'm going to give you my definition of what I mean when I say "competently" shortly.

So wrap your mind around this ...

Here's how I want you to envision something that you'd like to learn.

THE LEVELS OF LEARNING

L et's say that you want to learn business. First, I want you to think of business as a building.

Business of Mastery

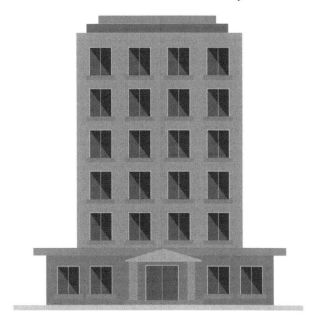

I want you to think of this building as having all these different floors that you've got to elevate to, and when you get to the next floor, you've elevated.

So you come into the building, and it's like a maze.

And the thing you've got to do is find the elevator. And in order to find the elevator, you've got to be observant. You've got to pay attention. And you've got to find all these clues.

So you go into the building, you start uncovering clues, and all of a sudden, you find the elevator.

But let's imagine that you've never seen an elevator before.

So this elevator, to you, just looks like a small room, but you know, based on all of the clues that you've gathered, that this is where you're supposed to go.

Now, you're looking around in this elevator thinking, *The thing that I'm looking for is not in this little room,* and you go in the elevator and the door gets ready to close and you jump off the elevator.

You jump off the elevator because you don't have a mental model for elevating to the next level.

You want to go to the next level, but you don't have a mental model for an elevator.

So you get back off the elevator.

This is exactly what happens to people over and over and over again in their lives when it comes to business.

They want to get to competency in business where they can be a successful business owner—that's what's on the top floor of this building—but they come in on the first floor, and they start looking around, and they have no skills.

They can't make any money because they don't understand what it takes to make money in business.

They don't understand marketing and they don't understand sales. They don't understand lead generation.

So they start uncovering these clues.

And once they get on the elevator, finally they say, *Okay, well it's obviously in here. Maybe once the door closes, that's when the clue will reveal itself.*

So the door closes, and all of a sudden you see the panel where you can push the button that says Level 2. You push the button to Level 2.

It goes up, the door opens, and you see you're in a completely different place. And now you've mastered Level 1.

By going on the elevator up to the next floor, you've mastered all the clues on the first floor.

And let's just call the first floor Sales.

The first floor was Sales.

The second floor will be Marketing.

The next floor might be Team Building, etc.

So now you get the mental picture of the building.

So the question then becomes ...

In my life, in my business, how do I learn faster?

You've Got to Eliminate to Elevate

Elevation is what you want, right?

You want to go higher and higher and higher, but you don't realize that you can't go higher and higher and higher if you keep everything that you had while you were on the lower level.

Sometimes going higher means you've got to let go of some things that you had when you were on a lower level.

You've got to learn to Eliminate to Elevate.

I once read that sacrifice is not giving up something that you desire; sacrifice is letting go of something of a lower nature so you can take hold of something of a higher nature. (I wish I could remember which book it was!)

I want you to think of accomplishing your business goal or your family goal or your spiritual goal, or whatever your goal is.

Maybe you are like me and you have a desire to elevate your golf goal. It doesn't matter what arena your goal is in.

This principle works for everything in life.

You've got to eliminate to elevate.

What does that mean?

Let me explain.

Eliminate Conflict

If you want to get to the next level in business, you've got to eliminate conflict. When I say conflict, oftentimes the conflict I'm talking about is internal conflict. And that internal conflict usually manifests itself as resistance.

Did you catch that?

Internal conflict usually manifests itself as resistance.

You resist the very thing that can take you to the next level.

As I said, you get on an elevator, and you've never been in an elevator before, so you just think it's a small room, and then the door starts closing. *Hey, why is this door trying to close? Why are they trapping me in this small room?*

Then you get off the elevator.

You have to eliminate the internal conflicts that manifest themselves as resistance to the things that you are learning. And you have to recognize the real meaning behind the resistance.

When you are getting ready to go up to the next level, you are going to experience resistance.

Sometimes it's going to show up as overwhelm.

What you don't realize is that overwhelm is like a rocket booster. When rockets take off, they take off in phases.

The first phase gets you out of the Earth's atmosphere, the next phase gets you into the stratosphere, and the next phase gets you into orbit.

What you've got to realize is that when you feel overwhelmed, you're feeling that way because you're about to go into the next phase.

Overwhelm is kind of like driving a car with an automatic transmission.

When you're going at a certain speed in a certain gear, the engine starts revving up. And what happens? You don't say: *Oh my goodness! My engine is about to blow!*

No, it just lets you know that the engine is about to change gears.

It's about to go into a higher gear.

When you start to feel overwhelmed, you start thinking, *Oh my goodness, this is too much! I don't know if I can take it! I just feel overwhelmed right now …*

But what you've got to understand is that when you start feeling those feelings, those feelings are nothing more than a sign that you are getting ready to shift into a higher gear.

When you start feeling "overwhelm," understand that overwhelm is not a sign that you should quit.

Overwhelm is a sign that you are about to level up.

You're getting ready to go to another level.

While resistance sometimes manifests as overwhelm, it can also manifest as judgment.

Judgment can manifest itself through your thinking that something is too difficult for you. Or sometimes judgment manifests as thinking something is too easy. If you find yourself thinking, *I don't know why I have to do this or that, I'm smarter than that,* that's resistance masked as judgment.

Do you realize there are things in your life right now that you think are too hard for you to do, and the truth is the only reason you think they're too hard is that you've never properly learned how to do them?

Do you realize there is nothing really that's hard to do?

What's hard is thinking about needing to do something that you don't know how to do, and feeling like you have to do it *before* you learn how to do it.

Let's say you don't know anything at all about computers. You just barely know how to turn one on. You've never sent an email, and all of a sudden, you decide: *I want to start building websites.*

As soon as you start learning all of the terminology, you begin to realize that people who create websites speak a totally different language. They're talking about Javascript and PHP and HTML and cascading style sheets and CSS and all this other stuff that you've got to have, like an index and a hosting account and a URL, and you suddenly feel like you're drowning.

That's because you're feeling like you have to learn how to swim after you jump in the water, and it doesn't work that way.

I promise you there's nothing that is too hard for you to learn—if you learn it in the manner that I am explaining to you.

Imagine yourself saying:

Okay, I'm going to have a breakthrough.

I'm going to learn the first part of this—this overwhelming thing.

I'm going to learn everything there is to learn on the first level.

And not only am I going to learn about *everything there is to learn on the first level …*

I'm going to learn how *to do everything I've learned on the first level …*

And then I'm not just going to learn how to do everything on the first level …

I'm going to actually physically go do *everything I've learned to do on the first level …*

And then I'm going to get on the elevator, I'm going to push the button, and I'm going to go up to the next floor.

And then I'm going to learn <u>about</u> everything there is to learn about on the second level …

And then I'm going to learn <u>how to do</u> everything I've learned about on the second level …

And then I'm actually going to <u>go do</u> everything I've learned on the second level …

Or I will learn how to make myself do it.

Then, I'm going to go up to the next level.

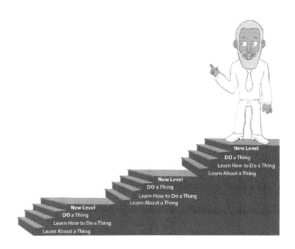

And I promise you, if you will learn like that, there's nothing that you cannot learn to the point of mastery, provided that it's within your physical capacity and mental capacity to do it.

What do I mean when I say, "within your mental and physical capacity to do it"?

Let me use myself as an example.

You see, I had polio as an infant, so now I wear a brace on my leg. I can learn as much about running as I'd like to learn, but it's not within my physical capacity to run. So I'm not going to win any footraces. I'm not going to be an Olympic runner because it is beyond my physical capacity.

The next thing you've got to do if you're going to eliminate conflict is you've got to recognize that all progress is not created equal.

And here's what that means ...

Some people feel as though busy-ness is productivity.

Busy-ness is not the same as productivity.

All movement is not progress.

You may be doing a lot of things in your business, and those things may not be working. That's because you've not mastered the lowest level of some of those things.

For instance, people want to master sales, but they haven't even mastered asking questions.

I'm going to give you a test right now. It's called "The Question Test." I want you to find somebody, one of your children, your spouse, somebody, and see how many questions in a row you can ask them.

Most people are so horribly inept at asking questions, yet they wonder why they can't sell.

You can't sell because you don't know anything about what the person is looking for because you can only ask one, two, or three questions. The conversation goes something like this:

"Hi, how are you today?"

"I'm fine."

"Great. So, um, what would you like to experience in your life?"

And they say this or that and you say, "Oh, okay."

You don't even know how to ask another question.

Question Asking is a level of mastery.

Listening to the Answers is a level of mastery.

All movement isn't progress. All busy-ness is not productivity.

Don't just run around the first floor of the building your entire life trying to hurry up and master it. Instead of moving really fast and accomplishing nothing, take time to truly master it.

In fact, take as much time as necessary to master it.

A lot of times we set goals and we set deadlines for those goals because the cultural indoctrination says: A goal is not a goal unless it has a deadline.

But sometimes, when you create a deadline, you create that deadline arbitrarily. You think, *I've got to learn this skill in this amount of time.*

What happens is once you reach the deadline, and you don't have that skill mastered, instead of stacking mastery on top of mastery, you're stacking *lack* of mastery on top of lack of mastery on top of lack of mastery. And then you get to a place in your business where the whole thing implodes.

Back to the building analogy …

Let's say you're at the bottom of the building, and before you even walk in the building, you look up and see it's 100 stories: *Oh man, I've got to master 100 things? I've got to master 100 to the point of effortlessness?*

Yes, you do.

But when you get to the top floor, all 100 of those things, even if you were doing them at the same time, would be as simple and as easy for you as tying your shoe.

What you've been taught your whole life is:

> You study this thing, and you get a good grade. And you study that thing, and you get a good grade. And you study that other thing, and you get a good grade. And you get recognized as being smart, and everything's going to be okay.

Or you've learned:

> You do step one, then you do step two, then you do step three, then you do step four, then you do step five, and now you can check all those things off because you've gotten them all done.

I'm not talking about getting things done.

I'm not talking about an artificial way of achieving something.

I'm talking about mastering everything to the point of not only *knowing* how to do it but also *doing it* so you can go to the next level and master those things.

And when you get to the top floor, you have stacked mastery on mastery so that when you do all those things that you've mastered effortlessly, other people look at you like you have superpowers.

So while it looks like you have some sort of superpower, you understand all the time and energy it took to master each one of those levels. You realize all of the hours of learning it took and then all of the hours of discipline to actually do those things. While things may look easy for you now, you know it wasn't nearly as easy for you to *learn* to do as it is for you *to do* them right now.

And by the way, it doesn't matter what you look at in your life. Everything in your life that comes easy to you now … none of it was as easy to learn to do as it is for you to do right now.

I remember the first time I cooked salmon. You know what I did? I got on YouTube. I watched a YouTube video. I watched about three or four YouTube videos. A couple of them I watched twice. And then I said, "Okay, I'm going to cook salmon."

Now I can cook salmon with my eyes closed. I already know what I'm going to do. I don't need a recipe. I don't need a measuring cup. I don't need a teaspoon. I don't need anything. I already know when I cook my salmon, it's going to be bad to the bone. Why? Because I've incrementally mastered cooking salmon to mastery. And it's so good, it'll make you hurt yourself—and the person sitting next to you.

Look, you've got to recognize that the elevator is not the destination.

The only purpose of an elevator is to get to the next level.

Don't make the mistake of thinking: *Okay, well, I've done all these things. I'm on the elevator. I've mastered this.*

You've got to understand that no matter what discipline you are seeking to master, they all have more than one floor.

I was reading Harry Barton's golf book, and he said that the average amateur golfer could be a scratch golfer in one year if they would learn to master one club at a time. That's so powerful.

Myron Golden says, "The average business owner could become a millionaire and build a very successful business if they'd master one business skill at a time."

Here's what happens …

When you start stacking one level you've mastered on top of another level you've mastered and another level on top of that, and you start stacking mastery on top of mastery on top of mastery … before you know it, you literally become one of the best in the world in your arena.

Why?

Because most people are unwilling to level up this way. Most people are unwilling to eliminate conflict. And most people are unwilling to eliminate cultural indoctrination.

Eliminate Cultural Indoctrination

You may be wondering, *What does cultural indoctrination have to do with mastery?* You will come to find out, everything! If you desire to go on to a higher level, you've got to eliminate cultural indoctrination because cultural indoctrination, for the most part, is designed to keep you stuck.

We are all influenced by cultural indoctrination.

I call it the "cultural hypnotic societal mechanism." The cultural hypnotic societal mechanism is a program. It's a program that's installed in our society as a whole. And that program is designed to keep us sick, broke, misinformed, and fearful.

It has a goal of making us *against* what's for us and *for* what's against us.

Did you catch that? If you didn't, go back and read that again.

Cultural indoctrination keeps you from so many of the things that you desire in life.

If you desire to elevate so that you can learn faster (and remember when I say "learn," I'm not just talking about knowing something—I'm talking about knowing about it, knowing how to do it, and then actually doing it), the first thing you've got to do is let go of cultural indoctrination.

So what does that look like?

Well, when you get ready to learn business, here's what cultural indoctrination says ...

Don't go into that building of being an entrepreneur. Don't go into that building because if you go into that building, there are no guarantees in that building.

Stay at your safe, secure job. Because if you go into that building of being an entrepreneur, what's going to happen is you're going to lose your security.

And remember cultural indoctrination tells us to go against what is for us, and go for what's against us. So to even get started, you've got to let go of cultural indoctrination.

I find it fascinating that people fill their minds with so much negativity all day, and they don't even understand that all of the mental and emotional energy that they give to the negativity is robbing them of the energy to take their life to a higher level.

So how do you eliminate cultural indoctrination?

You start by eliminating media.

Eliminate Media

The first step to eliminating cultural indoctrination is eliminating the media.

What do I mean by "the media"?

Stop watching the news and reading the newspaper. (I know I just lost some readers.)

You may be thinking, *What in the world is this guy talking about? You gotta read the paper! How will you know what's going on in the world?*

I've got a better question for you than that. If you can't fix what's going on in *your* world, how are you going to fix the problems going on in *the* world?

Here's the truth: If you desire to take your life to another level, you've got to let go of the baggage of media.

You've got to let go of the news.

You've got to let go of movies.

You've got to let go of television.

Let me tell you something. When I was broke, I didn't even have a television—not just cable television—*we didn't even have a television set.*

My children were teenagers by the time we started watching television. By then, we were financially independent.

You say, *Myron, what's your point?*

My point is you've got to understand something: Benjamin Franklin said that if you empty your purse into your mind, your mind will fill your purse with gold.

Myron Golden says, "Whoever puts the most money in your mind, that's who has most of your money."

And you can't compete with the advertisers on television.

You can't put as much money in your mind as they can through their television commercials. So what you've got to do is cut them off. Don't give them the opportunity to put anything in your mind.

If you are struggling financially, one of the worst things you can do is watch television.

Another one of the worst things you can do is listen to the news.

You're letting other people fill your mind.

You need to understand that your mind is a problem-solving mechanism. It's going to work on solving a problem, whether you desire it to or not. As soon as it finds a problem, it's going to go to work on it.

If you're filling up your mind with problems that you can't solve, you're wasting creative energy that you could be using to solve problems you *can* solve.

So you've got to cut off the media.

Is it necessary?

No, but I would highly recommend it unless, of course, you don't have any desire to elevate.

If you desire to elevate, there are some things you've got to eliminate—and the first thing to eliminate is the media.

Eliminate Minutiae

The next thing you've got to eliminate is minutiae.

You might be thinking, *Minutiae? What is this guy talking about?*

When I say minutiae, I'm talking about conversations about things that don't affect your life.

I can remember being in elementary school (now, keep in mind, I've been a little odd my whole life, so, you know, it is what it is) and hearing elementary school students talking about all of the stats of professional baseball players and professional football players and professional basketball players.

They knew all the stats of these people who didn't even know they existed.

I was like, *I don't get it.*

It didn't make any sense to me.

Even in elementary school, I thought: *Why would you spend that much of your life, that much of your mental capacity, your mental bandwidth to memorize stats about somebody who probably wouldn't even wave hello to you if you said hi to him?*

95

That's *never* made sense to me.

We spend our lives thinking that we're supposed to talk about all of the stuff that *they* (the cultural hypnotic societal mechanism) tell us to.

Let me give you a specific example …

While playing nine holes of golf with a friend of mine, he said something that was really fascinating to me.

And, please, don't take this the wrong way. I mean, I feel for anybody's family who loses a loved one.

But he said, "Man, we're losing all of these singers this year." And then he said, "We lost Prince."

And I'm thinking to myself, *What does that mean? How did* we *lose him?*

Don't get me wrong, I feel sadness for his family and for the families of anybody who loses a loved one. I feel that.

But …

We put so much stock in things that don't affect us.

It doesn't compute for me.

We have far too many conversations about things that don't affect us. And we have far too many conversations about things we can't affect.

We buy into this idea that somehow we have to have conversations about things like Prince dying. So now I've got to spend hours and hours trying to figure out how he died. I've got to have conversations with people about it over and over and over again.

Why? I believe it's because we have been subconsciously focusing on distractions and not focusing on things that make a difference in our lives and the lives of the people we are supposed to be serving.

Yes, it's sad when someone dies. Yes, it's sad when a celebrity dies. But focusing on that doesn't give us the ability to make anyone's life better.

I don't mean to minimize death, but I do want you to understand that those kinds of conversations are taking up far too much bandwidth in your mind.

If you figure out how he died, it's not going to add anything to your life.

You've got to eliminate things that are minor in relation to how to take your life to another level.

Because if you truly understood what going to another level means, you would stop wasting your creative energy on things that you can't control.

I hope you are picking up what I'm putting down!

Eliminate Interruptions

So, you've got to eliminate the media, you've got to eliminate the minutia, and the next thing you've got to eliminate is interruptions.

And not just external interruptions ...

You've got to eliminate internal interruptions.

One of the reasons that most business-opportunity seekers never do well in their business is that they are always changing gears.

They'll find all these clues and get really, really close to the elevator and somebody will say, "Hey, did you know that ..."

And the next thing you know, they are off in a totally different direction: *I'm going to go do this for a while.*

They do the new thing until it feels to them like it's *not working*.

In reality, though, when most business-opportunity seekers, entrepreneurs, or up-and-coming entrepreneurs come to the conclusion that "this is not working," they don't have any idea of what "working" looks like or feels like, so they don't actually know if it's working or not.

Cultural indoctrination would have you believe if it doesn't feel right, it's not right.

Not only is that not correct, it's the complete opposite.

Change in the right direction
feels wrong in the moment.

One of the very first things that I share with all of my coaching clients is this:

When I am coaching you, almost everything that I tell you to do—the things that will take your life to another level—will feel wrong to you.

It's going to be very counterintuitive to you. Because if it felt intuitive, if it felt right, you would already be doing it.

Do you understand that, right now, all of the things that can take your life to another level financially, to another level in your business—all of those things—don't feel like they would work?

If you started doing them, you'd say: *Nah, it can't be that.* And the reason you're saying "it can't be that" is because you don't even understand what it really is to experience that next-level breakthrough. You don't even have a frame of reference for it.

You could be staring it in the face.

You could be wallowing in it and not even know it.

You've got to understand that if you're not living life at a level that you desire, and you're not experiencing life in your business or in your family or in your spirituality at a level that you desire— that maybe, just maybe, your current perspective is off.

By the way, this doesn't make you foolish, nor does it make you a bad person. When you become aware of the fact that, "Hey, I've been working on this thing my whole life and it's not working," *maybe* the reason it's not working is that you don't know what "working" really is.

So let me tell you what "working" really is. Work is a two-sided coin. When the two-sided coin called "work" lands on heads, it's working for me. This is the work that feels right and pays lots of money and people celebrate us for.

But when the two-sided coin of work lands on tails, it's not working *for* us. But it's working *on* us. When you realize this, you will come to the understanding that there is no such thing as work that doesn't work.

All work works; it's either working for me, or it's working on me.

When you really get this, you'll stop becoming disillusioned and thinking that something isn't working just because it's not working for you at the moment. The work that you are working on that's not working for you will work on you until you become the person for whom it can work.

This understanding will keep you from quitting three feet from gold like the story in the book *Acres of Diamonds* tells us about.

Eliminate Confusion

The next thing that you've got to eliminate to elevate is confusion.

When I say confusion, I'm talking about a lack of clarity.

Confusion is oftentimes manifested as a lack of clarity, and a lack of clarity is a result of not attaining mastery at the level you're on right now.

In other words, you've got a bunch of different things that you know are essential, and you know about *where* they are, you know about *what* they are, and you kind of understand a little bit of *how* to use them. Then you grab all the stuff that's incomplete and you jump on the elevator.

Eliminating confusion is simple: *Master* one level before moving to another level.

Here is the thing you have to understand: Mastery does not always come from being told a step-by-step process. Mastery can come from the wisdom you gain while you are in the *process* of *doing* the thing.

Again, you have to understand that eliminating confusion does not always come from being given a step-by-step process.

It's so funny to me that the students want to teach the teacher how to teach them: *Tell me Step 1, then tell me Step 2, then tell me Step 3, then tell me Step 4, then tell me Step 5.*

Sometimes it doesn't work like that.

Here is what I recommend: When you buy a new home study course, a new program, go through the entire thing without attempting to put any of it into play. Just go through the entire thing.

Don't take notes. Don't do anything. Just listen. Just watch. Just read.

Familiarize yourself with it, and then go back through it, attempting to implement. Understand that until you can do it, you do not know it.

Knowing about something is not the same as knowing something.

What happens if you've got a lack of clarity and you stack a lack of clarity on top of another lack of clarity on top of another lack of clarity on top of another lack of clarity … By the time you get up to the eighth floor, you can't even see anymore.

Everything's blurry.

It's like you have cataracts.

You can't see what's going on around you because you didn't use "segmentation to completion." Segmentation to completion is a high achievement success principle successful people use to accomplish more in a day than many people do in an entire week. It means to work on one project at a time, read one book at a time.

Finish what you start before you start something new.

When you apply this principle to your life and business, at first it feels like you are not making much progress, but by the time you get to the end and you don't have to go back and do things over, you will see how much more you are getting done in less time.

Eliminate the Need to Be Right

The last thing you need to eliminate is the need to be right.

The biggest hindrance to learning is thinking that you already know.

What you've got to do is get over the need to get an A on your report card. I understand we were programmed to want to get the A, but all of us have got to get over it.

Get over your need to be right, because people who have to be right find it very hard to get rich.

So you might as well decide right now:

**Would you rather be right,
or would you rather be rich?**

INCREMENTAL MASTERY TO EFFORTLESSNESS

Model the Success You Wish to Achieve

One time I went to visit my daughter in Pennsylvania, and I ended up taking some shooting lessons from my son-in-law. He was in the military, and he was an expert marksman.

My daughter asked, "Dad, you want to go shooting?"

I said, "Sure." Then I said, "I'm going to be really good at this."

And my wife and my daughter laughed at me. They said, "Have you ever shot a gun before?"

I said, "No."

"Then, how can you know you're gonna be good at it?"

"Because I know how to learn things."

And so, before we ever left the house, I said to my son-in-law, "Okay, tell me everything you believe about shooting a gun." And he told me everything he believed.

When we got to the shooting range, I said, "Okay, tell me how to hold the gun. Tell me how to stand, tell me how to breathe, tell me everything I'm supposed to do physically."

You want to model three things from the person who has achieved the level of success you wish to achieve.

First, you model their belief systems.

Next, you model their physiology.

And the last thing you model is their mental syntax, or the order in which they fire off messages in their brain.

It's not enough to do the right things when you are leveling up. To experience a breakthrough, you have to do the right things in the right order.

The first time I ever went shooting with a handgun, I put four bullets in the same hole. Why? Because I modeled somebody who was good at it.

I didn't bring any of my beliefs about shooting a gun to the range with me. I chucked my beliefs, and I took on the beliefs of the guy who knew what he was doing.

When you desire to learn a new thing, you've got to trust the person's belief system that you are modeling more than you trust in your own belief system.

For example, as a golfer, I might have a belief that "hitting a driver straight is hard." That belief may be true for me, based on what I know about hitting a driver.

But if I ask a person who's really, really good at golf, "Hey, do you think hitting a driver straight is hard?"

If that person says, "No I don't," then I'm going to say, "Tell me everything you believe about hitting a driver."

If you desire to duplicate any form of human excellence, find somebody who is experiencing excellence in that arena and then model that.

It's amazing to me how some golfers never level up.

Golfers are fascinating people because they don't even know why what they are doing isn't working but they *think* they know.

Golfers are the worst self-diagnostic people on the planet. They're thinking, *Oh, I need to pick up my head.* Or, *Oh, I'm swinging too fast.*

What most golfers assign as the reason that they didn't hit the golf ball properly isn't the real reason they didn't hit the ball well.

Now, I don't know everything about golf, but I've studied it extensively. I used to coach high school golf, and I'm a fairly good golf teacher.

All of the things that most golfers assign as the reasons that they don't hit the golf ball properly are almost always wrong because they're basing them on the mental model that they have—and the mental model that they have is wrong.

For instance, if you're going to hit an iron, you hit an iron with a downward motion to make the ball go up in the air.

Most amateur golfers try to scoop it because the club has an angle.

So they try to scoop it, and they don't even understand that the reason they keep hitting the ball fat and then thin and then fat and then thin is that they're trying to scoop it.

Their mental model is wrong.

They haven't leveled up to the basics—they haven't even finished the first-floor level yet.

I'm telling you ... there are so many things in your life that are like that. If you take time to master the things on your current level, you will get to go to the elevator and go up to the next level.

And when you master the things on that level, you get to go up to the next level.

When I say "master," I mean:

1) You know what they are,

2) You know how to do them, and

3) You do them effortlessly.

Here's how you can tell if you've really learned how to do something ...

If you can do it as simply as tying your shoes, you've learned it. Because how much effort do you put into that? You don't put any effort into it.

Why?

Because you've mastered it.

And how do you do that?

Incremental mastery to effortlessness.

When you get to a point of effortlessness, that is another level. That's when you know how to do the things, you know what they are, and you do them effortlessly.

When you master things at that level, you never think "close enough" is close enough or "good enough" is good enough. At that point, you have mastered everything that can be mastered on each level.

What happens when you get to the top level?

Now you've got all this mastery and you are experiencing business from a place of effortlessness.

When you reach effortlessness, you will struggle to wrap your mind around the idea that there's difficulty in things that other people are trying really, really hard to do, and struggling to do ... even though, while you were leveling up, you experienced a level of difficulty and struggle as well.

The Creative Process to Productivity

I love studying the Bible. Everything I teach about business, I either found in the Bible or I confirmed in the Bible because the Bible is the best business book known to mankind.

If I get business principles from somewhere else, I always go to the Bible to make sure that they line up with the Bible.

Why?

Because the Bible is already proven to be factual for me and my life. That's not me trying to push my beliefs off on you, but just so you know, that's where I'm coming from.

Genesis Chapter 1 says that in the beginning, God created the heavens and the earth. And it says he did this on day one ... and the evening and the morning were the first day ... and then on day two God created the firmament, and he called the firmament Heaven ... and the evening and the morning were the second day ... and then on day three ...

God could have just said that he created the heavens and the earth and all the animals and all the people and all the stuff in seven days. He could have said that, but he didn't say that.

Why didn't he say that?

The reason he didn't say that is because the very first thing that God tells us about God is that he is creative.

And the very first thing that God tells us about us is that he created us in his image, which means he created us to be creative.

You see, when God created everything out of nothing in seven days, he created three categories in creation.

1. He created creation—the sun, the moon, the grass, and the trees, etc.

2. He created creatures—dogs, cats, alligators, and giraffes, etc.

3. He created creators—humans.

God created us to create things and he made us to make things.

You say, what does that have to do with anything?

That's why I believe he went into so much detail about how he created everything, so that as the creators that he designed us to be, we would have a mental model. We'd have a process of productivity. And if we go through these steps of productivity, that will give us the ability to create like he created, using the same process.

So here's what I mean …

It says, in the beginning, God created the heavens and the earth.

The first thing that comes in the creative process—the very first step in the creative process—is intention.

God created the heavens and the earth:

That is intention.

The next thing that happens is disruption.

111

And the earth was without form and void and darkness was upon the face of the deep.

The word "was" that is used in this passage is the word "became," so the earth became without form and void. (A lot of scholars believe that Satan attempted to destroy the earth that God created after God kicked him out of heaven.)

So there's disruption.

Why is this important?

God's showing us that just because we intend to create something doesn't mean there's not going to be any interruption or disruption.

Disruption is a natural part of the creative process.

What comes after that?

Inspiration to create.

The spirit of God moved upon the face of the waters, and God said, "Let there be light."

That's illumination.

And then it goes on to say that the evening and the morning were the first day.

That's segmentation to completion.

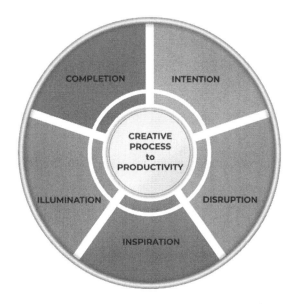

And the evening and the morning were the first day.

And then it says, and God saw the light, that it was good.

Observation: taking in what you've created.

So you say, *Myron, what's your point?*

My point is that when you have mastered something to completion, the process is totally clear and it seems effortless.

It may look hard to other people, but because you have mastered it, you don't so much think about what you are doing, you are just doing it.

For example, I was teaching at a leadership conference, and a gentleman came up and said, "Man, I can't write that fast. Can I have your notes?"

And I said, "I don't actually use notes. Sorry." I didn't have any notes to share. I don't use notes because I have clarity. Now, don't get me wrong, I understand that you can use notes and still have clarity, but the more clarity you have, the less you need notes.

Think about it, you don't need notes to ride a bike. You don't need notes to tie your shoes. Why don't you need notes? The reason you don't need notes is because you've mastered those activities.

One of the reasons I speak so clearly is because when I process information, I don't just process it to know about it. I process it to know how to do it and then to know how to make myself do it so that I have that mastery.

So when I'm talking to you about something, it's not theory. It's something that I actually do.

We've got to have a level of clarity that allows us to proceed without stumbling. That's why we don't want to say, "Okay, well, that's close enough."

Close enough is not close enough. In a 500-piece puzzle, 496 pieces in the puzzle are not enough. We want completion.

Like putting together a puzzle to completion, clarity doesn't always come through a step-by-step process.

Total clarity in the business that you desire to go into—whether it be real estate, internet marketing, consulting, online courses, or whatever it is—only comes at the top floor.

And what you've got to do is to master each one of those floors along the way.

The only way you know if you've mastered them is this: As you are learning the things to do, you actually begin to do them.

Otherwise, reading the book or listening to the modules only gives you the ability to know *about* it.

Understand that total clarity in the overall business itself only comes on the top floor, and you can only get to the top floor *after* you've mastered the things on every individual floor below it.

The objective is not just movement: *Well, I'm doing a lot of stuff.*

The objective of mastery is incremental improvement to effortlessness. That's right, "mastery" is the end game. But it is accomplished incrementally. You learn and practice (that's incremental), and learn and practice, and learn and practice.

Then, all of a sudden, one day, you don't have to learn and practice.

You can just do it.

PARTNERSHIPS, PURPOSE, AND PRIORITIES

Partnerships in Business

Someone once asked me how to scale a custom software business for a well-established start-up. So I shared the principle of partnerships, which again, I got from the Bible because the Bible has a lot to say about partnerships: Two are better than one and a three-fold cord is not quickly broken. In other words, there is strength in numbers. Besides, while it's true that we are all good at something, it is also true that none of us are good at everything,

I told him that Russell Brunson, who is the co-founder of Click-Funnels and a serial entrepreneur who started his first online company while still in college, is the best person in the world to model on how to build and scale a software business.

Russell built a software system and created a course to teach people how to grow their businesses. He sells them the course and then gives them the software free for 30 days. After they are using the software successfully, they don't want to stop using it.

The educational course is the front end that only exists for the purpose of getting people hooked on the software on the back end.

By the way, it doesn't matter what business you have or what business you're in, the best front end for any business is an information product that educates people on how to use the solution you provide.

Make your main thing your back end, and create an information product for the front end. It will change the game for you.

If you're the developer, in order to scale, find and partner with a marketing person who's great at marketing. Let them be what Russell calls "the dancing monkey" and you become a partner. Let them blow it up to a billion dollars.

You be the Steve Wozniak. Let a partner play the part of Steve Jobs.

You be the Todd Dickerson, and find yourself a Russell Brunson.

Stop selling your services and partner with somebody who could help you take that thing up to a hundred million dollars. That's what I would do.

If you don't like partners or have had bad experiences with them, then you just haven't found the right partner yet.

I don't like bad partners either, but I love great partners.

I am going to give you a principle of partnership. We are in the partnership age, whether you know it or not.

Let me show you what I mean by that.

Apple became the number one market cap company in the world

because of what they created in 2008. They created the iPod in 2001, the iPhone in 2007, and the iPad in 2010. So what did Apple create in 2008? They created the App Store. The App Store was Apple's new partnership platform.

Apple created a platform and then for the first time in history, a multi-billion dollar company (then, and now a multi-trillion dollar company), decided to give people partnership agreements instead of just giving them a job. And Apple said to these new partners, "If you will create apps for our App Store or books for our bookstore, we will pay you 70% and we will keep 30%."

You may be one of those people who doesn't want to give up 30%–50% of your business to a partner. But the most successful company in American history is willing to give up 70%.

That is what catapulted them past ExxonMobil.

Why?

Because they weren't just hiring people to do work for them.

They said to average, ordinary people, "We have a billion-dollar company. If you will create content for our customers, we will give you 70% of the profits."

I was teaching this concept on partnerships at a church one day, and as I was teaching on Proverbs 30:27 which says, "The locusts have no king, yet go they forth all of them by bands," I was describing the wisdom of cooperation from the locusts.

Then, I started talking about all the verses in scripture that taught cooperation and participation: Two are better than one (Ecc. 4:9)

... a threefold cord is not quickly broken (Ecc. 4:12) ... For where two or three are gathered together in my name, there am I in the midst of them (Matt. 18:20) ... How should one chase a thousand, and two put ten thousand to flight (Deut. 32:30)?

Wait a minute.

If one will chase a thousand, why won't two chase two thousand?

I thought that said ten thousand.

Oh! It *did* say ten thousand!

Myron's math would say: If one would chase one thousand, two would chase two thousand.

God's math says if one will chase one thousand, two will chase ten thousand.

Those are war terms, but because all principles are microcosms of each other, let's translate it into wealth terms:

If one person can make $1,000, then two people can make $10,000.

As soon as I saw that, I said, "Wait a minute, 50% of 10,000 is 5 times more than 100% of 1,000."

50% of 10,000 = 5,000

100% of 1,000 = 1,000

At that moment, I realized that for the rest of my life ...

I would rather have 50% of a watermelon than 100% of a grape.

Purpose of Business

I believe that the purpose of all of our lives, the solution to all our problems and all the economic problems in the world … is found in Matthew 6:33. It says, "But seek ye first the Kingdom of God, and his righteousness; and all these things shall be added unto you."

Almost no one knows what that means. In America, we sure don't know what it means because we don't live in a kingdom. We don't know what a kingdom is. We don't know what a kingdom does.

We live in a democratic republic (for the time being at least … they're trying to turn it into a socialistic society, but that's another

121

conversation for another day). We live in a democratic republic. We don't know how a kingdom operates.

In a kingdom, people grow up in a monarchy and understand that everything and everyone in the kingdom already belongs to the Royal Family.

So when it says, "seek ye first the Kingdom of God," the word kingdom means "king's dominion."

The best definition of kingdom that I've ever found is that *I yield my life to God as the sovereign King of my life,* which means He's in control of Myron. Myron's not in control of Myron. That's number one. And I yield—not surrender. *Yield.*

Surrender is something you do to a foe or an enemy. Yielding is something you can do to a friend.

When I yield to God as the sovereign King of my life, I get to become the sovereign king over an assignment.

When I yield to God, my assignment has to yield to me. I don't have to wonder if it's going to work if I'm yielding. I know it's going to work.

Why?

I'm yielding to him. It has to yield to me. Then, I use the assignment that I rule over to serve the people I come into contact with.

That is the kingdom of God in a nutshell. Those are the practices of someone operating within the kingdom of God.

Now, we get a choice. We can choose to operate within the kingdom of God, or if we choose not to, then we are by default choosing to operate within the kingdom of God's adversary, Satan.

To help you understand this better, let me explain the differences between the two kingdoms.

The principles of the kingdom of God are freedom, profits, abundance, and life.

The principles of the kingdom of Satan are wages, slavery, lack, and death.

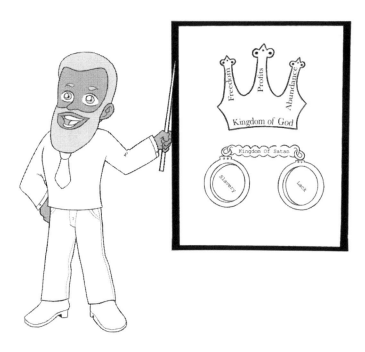

God is a king who, when you yield to his authority, will make you a king or a queen and bless you with life. Satan is a fake king. When you yield to his authority, he will make you a slave and when he's used you up, he will kill you or leave you for dead. He will try to get you to be a slave who's attempting to rule over other people and use those people to serve you "stuff."

I am telling you, the most fulfilling, purposeful place you will ever find yourself in life is being yielded to the God of the Bible as the sovereign king of your life.

If you're wondering, *Why is Myron talking about religion?* I'm not talking about religion because the Bible is not a religious book. I know that might be hard for you to believe, but stick with me. Yes, the Bible talks about religion, but God didn't start religions. That's another conversation that we don't have time to get into right now.

But here is what God's Kingdom says: Yield your life to God as the sovereign king of your life, and rule over the assignment as a sovereign king of that assignment, and then use that assignment that you rule over to serve everybody you come in contact with.

If everybody on planet earth did that, this world would be hopping and popping. There would not be a single solitary war. There would be no poverty. It would solve all those problems.

But here's the problem with people: People decide before they discern. What do I mean? They decide what to do before they discern what they're supposed to do.

The only way to discover what God created you to do is to yield to it before you know what it is. If you're truly yielded to your purpose and you're seeking to serve other people, God's not going to leave you hanging.

The second thing to think about is what you are good at and what you like to do because when you find the thing that you're good at, *and* the thing you like to do, *and* it solves a problem for other people ... that's your sweet spot.

I know how to do a lot of things. For example, I know how to build a sales funnel, but I don't like doing it, so I pay other people to do it. I know how to do a webinar, but I don't like to do webinars either. I just don't enjoy it.

My sweet spot is having conversations with people, teaching them how the world works, how business works, and how money works from God's perspective—because whether you believe it or not, that's the only perspective that really matters. And he won't be offended and his feelings won't even be hurt a little if you don't believe it. Neither are mine.

My advantage in the marketplace is I see things from God's perspective because I've been studying the Bible for 44 years—since I was 16 years old. And I've not been studying it for what to do from a religious perspective. I've been looking for my orders from headquarters for what I'm supposed to do with my life.

How I'm supposed to treat people.

How I'm supposed to use my money.

How I'm supposed to treat my wife.

How I'm supposed to treat my children.

How I'm supposed to treat my parents.

How I'm supposed to treat my siblings.

How I'm supposed to treat strangers.

I'm getting my orders from headquarters.

So that's the second thing, figuring out what you like to do.

One of my sweet spots is teaching the Bible. Another sweet spot is teaching business. Another is selling from the stage. When I combine all that together I'm doing something I like to do. It serves people, and it makes me a decent living.

God is not religious; God is the creator of government. He creates laws that govern the universe. The Bible is a book about governments, not a book about religion. There are religions in it, yes, but it's not a religious book.

Satan started the first religion, and then all the other religions came from that, and that religion was humanism or hedonism— "and you shall be as gods knowing good and evil" (Gen. 3:5). So humanism says you can do "this or that" to be more like God or you've got to do "this or that" to be accepted by God, but all you really have to do is yield to God.

Priorities in Business

My philosophy for business is threefold. I'm going to give them to you in order of priority, not the order of importance. The order of priority is the exact reverse order of the order of importance.

I don't want to do the most important things first. I want to do the first things first. If I attempt to do the most important things first, my business is going to fail.

Leverage

My first priority in business is leverage. What is leverage? Leverage is a device or mechanism that allows me to produce a multiplied output from minimal input. I put in a little bit, but I get a lot out.

When you find leverage, you put in minimal input that produces maximum output. Unfortunately, most people are putting a lot in and getting a little out. That's called reverse leverage. You don't want to do that.

Some of the best advice I can give you is either you figure out how to use leverage, or someone is going to figure out how to use you as their leverage. So you had better figure out how to use leverage.

Most people think they're limited by their limited ability. The reason God gave you a limited ability was so that you'd be smart enough to find some leverage.

One of my favorite scientific wealth principles is that I can always make up in leverage what I lack in ability. If I'm not good at something, great. I don't have to be good at it. I'll find leverage.

For example, there's this woman on my team named Lorrinda— and she lives in North Carolina (I live in Florida). She is brilliant at a level that I cannot comprehend. She is good at everything I'm bad at.

She came to me and said, "Myron, I want to work for you."

I said, "That's nice. I'm not hiring."

In the past, I've had flaky people want to work with me, and I give them something to do and then they flake out three days later. They would say, "I can't do it," or "I had a nervous breakdown," or something.

So she said, "That's okay. I'll work for you for free."

I wondered what I could give her to make her go away so I would never hear from her again. That was my mentality. I wasn't trying to be mean, that was just where I was at.

So I figured I would give her something so hard that she'd decide that she doesn't want to work for me.

She had come to me right after our Stripe account got shut down. Our continuity program had grown to 500 members at that time. Stripe had given us just seven days to find a new merchant provider, and at this point, I was willing to just shut it down so I didn't have to deal with it.

I told her we need to move all these people off this payment platform onto this other payment platform.

We need to enter their card information, and if they don't have it, call them so we can still collect money.

She said okay.

I was thinking, *I'll never hear from her again.* Remember, I would have rather shut the membership program down before I did all of that myself. I had already decided that I wasn't going to do it.

I woke up the next morning with all these emails from her in the middle of the night with updates: "This is what I've got done so far … This is what I'm doing next …This is what I'm working on now."

This thing I thought was going to drive her away, she got done in two days working on it all night long. I'm thinking, *Who is this person? Who does that?* I don't stay up all night working for my own business, I don't care how bad the crisis is.

She did that, so I said, "Cool. I'm going to hire you one day a week."

She was getting more done in a day in administration and operations than I could get done in a week. Meanwhile, because

I was only paying her for one day a week, she was doing sub-contract work for other people.

I'm thinking, *I do not want this woman to get away.*

So I said to her, "What's it going to take for you to stop working for all of those other people and just work for me?"

I'm a very frugal businessman. I'm not one of these people who just blows hundreds of thousands of dollars a month on Facebook ads. Our net profit margins are crazy high because I am frugal.

I only net pay myself $3,822.91 a week. I don't need any more than that (the truth is I don't need that much, but my accountant says I can't pay myself less because according to the IRS, it wouldn't be "reasonable compensation"). I make approximately $16K a month gross as a W-2 employee of my own business. We consistently make 6 and sometimes even 7 figures a month, but regardless of what the business makes, I still make $16K per month.

I'm frugal.

Why? I know what it feels like to be broke, and I don't like the feeling. You know what's worse than the feeling of being broke? Feeling broke because you were rich and lost it all!

I'm going to stay as far away from broke as I can. If I can keep broke as far from my life as Los Angeles is from New York City, I'm going to do it.

Let's get back to Lorrinda. I said to her, "What's it going to take for you to stop working for all of those other people and just work for me?"

She said, "Well, I used to be in corporate America. I was making $300,000 a year."

I thought, *Oh brother, here it comes.*

"When I worked in corporate America, I paid off my house, I paid off my car, I paid off my mom's house. I don't really need much money. You pay me $1,000 per month, and I'll work for you full-time."

And I said, "I'm frugal, but I'm not cheap."

So I started her out at a little more than that. Not much more than that, but a little more than that. She makes more now per week than she made per month when she first came to work with us (that doesn't even include bonuses). I gave her an incentive, and when she achieved it, she got another raise. In addition to the raise, she became an equity partner in my business.

This woman is bad to the bone. I don't have to wonder if things will get done. She's created Trello boards, Slack plates, and whatever else that stuff is. I was on Trello one time and I was like, "Oh, that's nice." I don't know how to do any of that stuff.

I find people who are good at what I'm bad at, who play at what I work at, and I pay them to do it so I don't have to.

I have five full-time employees on my team. I've got seven sub-contractors. Our monthly payroll, not including my sales guy, is a little over $60K per month. That includes my salary. We're lean and mean.

I submit to you that you should run a lean and mean business.

I'm going to give you some business advice that'll help you stay in business for a long time.

Learn from me because I made all the stupid mistakes that you can make when you're young and in business making and spending a lot of money.

Here's what you do.

To run your business lean and mean, hire a payroll company. Become a W-2 employee of your own business. Have them cut your paycheck and your employees' paychecks. Pay your taxes quarterly. Set up a pension plan for yourself, and be smart with your money as a business owner.

Live a simple life.

You don't need a Lamborghini or a Bentley or a Rolls Royce. You don't need a Mercedes. You don't. Unless you are going to use those things to make more money.

They're nice and I have that stuff, but it's not necessary.

Set your business up to win first.

Put your business in a place where your business can't lose, then go get your toys. Get toys from the overflow.

You'll be so glad if you decide to run your business lean and mean.

If you become a W-2 employee of your own business, you don't have to worry about the IRS or somebody coming and making your business go away.

You're set up for the rest of your life.

It's something like $6,000 a year people can put in an IRA, right? We have a pension plan that's so good that my business can contribute $390,000 per year.

I don't have to pay taxes on that money until I take it out.

If I didn't put the money in the pension plan, I'd have to send it to the IRS.

I can borrow money from the pension plan if I want to. I don't need to, but if I want to, I can.

And if the IRS comes and says, "Well, you owe us a lot of money," they can't take my money out of my pension plan because the penalties will be too high.

Be smart in your business. Hire people. I have a tax attorney who is brilliant. I have an accountant who is brilliant. I've got a sales guy who is brilliant. I've got an operations manager who is brilliant.

My business partners are my family. My wife, my son, my daughter, and my son-in-law. Even my two-year-old grand-daughter owns part of our family business. We are all partners. It's a *we* business, not a *me* business.

We've got a business that's tighter than Fort Knox.

I recommend you do the same thing.

Lifestyle

After leverage in my business, my second priority is lifestyle.

What does lifestyle mean? It means different things to different people. To me it means going to play golf before I work, so when I'm at work, I'm not thinking about being at the golf course.

It means being able to play with my granddaughter anytime I want to.

It means being able to go on a world-class vacation with my wife any time we want as many times as we want—five, six, seven, eight, nine times a year.

It means when we go on vacation to Israel, if we want to, I can take my brother, who is a pastor, his wife, and their 16-year-old daughter with us. That's lifestyle.

Lifestyle should be your second priority in business.

Your thing might be fishing, or going to baseball games. It might be reading books. Figure out what lifestyle means to you and do that.

Do something to reward yourself for all of this grinding and hustling you're doing. Why? It will incentivize you to go do it some more. Life is too long to work hard and not play hard. But it's a paradox. Because life is also too short to work hard and not to play hard.

So many people hustle and grind and hustle and grind and say they are going to get to the lifestyle later, and then they die and, oops, they forgot to get to the lifestyle. It's over and they never got to enjoy the things they wanted to.

I'm going to tell you something that is more important than what you do for a living: what you do while you're living.

The quality of your life is not measured by the number of years of experience you have doing a thing. The quality of your life is measured by the number of experiences you put in your years.

That's what I mean when I say lifestyle.

Some people say: *Time is money.*

When someone tells me "time is money," I immediately know three things about them. I know they don't understand time, they have no earthly idea about money, and they're broke.

Rich people understand that time is not money. We understand that time is infinitely more valuable than money.

Poor people waste a whole lot of time trying to save a little bit of money.

Rich people invest as much money as necessary so we can buy back the rest of our lives.

Time is not money.

Time is infinitely more valuable than money.

When you learn to value time more than you value money, then you can get rich.

Why?

Because wealth is measured more in time than it is in money.

What do I mean by that?

Most people make the mistake of attempting to measure wealth just in money, but if you're going to really measure wealth, you've also got to measure it in time.

Here's what I mean …

If I make $1 million, am I rich? The answer is, it depends.

Here's what it depends on: Time.

If I work for 40 years and I make $25,000 a year, I made $1 million.

Am I rich?

No.

Why?

Because it took me too long to make it.

What if I make $1 million in the next 12 months?

Now, am I rich?

Yes.

I may not be Big Rich, but at least I'm rich, right?

These two people made the same amount of money. One of them just made it 40 times faster.

The difference between creating wealth and not creating wealth is not just money but also speed.

Wealth has a need for speed.

You know why most people are broke?

We've been warned our entire lives about "get-rich-quick schemes," but nobody's ever warned us about the "stay-broke-for-the-rest-of-our-lives" scheme that we've already bought into.

Are you picking up what I'm putting down?

If you've got a money problem, your money problem is not that you don't make enough money—it's that you make money too slowly.

If you take the amount of money you make every year and you start making that amount every month, then you're good.

Take the amount of money you make every month and start making that amount of money every week and you're better.

Take the amount of money you make every week and start making that amount of money every day.

You're going to be alright!

I remember in the '80s, I didn't make $4,000 in a whole year. I was broke. I wasn't just poor, I was "pitiful poor." You say: *Myron, what's pitiful poor?* That's when you're so poor, poor people feel sorry for you.

Now, sometimes I make more money in an hour than I used to make in an entire decade.

What was the difference-maker?

The difference-maker was me.

I finally became the person who could do the thing, so I could have the stuff.

That's what you've got to learn to do.

Legacy

The third and last priority, and the most important reason my business exists, is for legacy.

What is legacy? Legacy is about not making the next generation start over from scratch.

I didn't want my children to have to start from scratch like I did.

Some people say, "I don't want my children to have it easy. I want them to have it hard like I did, because that made me what I am."

First of all, you don't know what made you what you are.

And second of all, that's as dumb as a box of rocks.

Yes, I have some opinions, and eventually, I'll work up enough courage to express them!

I happen to believe the Bible is the ultimate truth.

You can believe that or not believe it. I'm not here to attempt to get you to believe it. That's just where I'm coming from.

The scripture tells me that a good man leaves an inheritance to his children's children, so if I want to consider myself to be a good man, I've got to leave an inheritance, not just to my children, but also to their children.

I don't want my children to start over. I don't want my grand-children to start over. I don't want my great-grandchildren to start over. That's why our business produces multiple 6 figures and 7 figures a month.

My lifestyle only costs me $5,000 a month to live. That's it. Now, I make more than $5,000 a month, but all of my payroll for my business and all my business expenses every month are minuscule compared to the amount of revenue we bring in. Why?

Because I'm not making this money just so I can have a nice car or have a nice house or go on a nice vacation. That's not the only thing. Get that stuff out of the way so you can start building a legacy.

My daughter and my son-in-law didn't have to start from scratch. My son didn't have to start from scratch. Their children won't have to start from scratch.

I'm not building this wealth for myself. I get to enjoy it, but it's not just for me, it's for generations.

It's for me, in my lifetime, to impact my family first, my community second, the world third, and for me to give them the ability to do the exact same thing.

That's legacy.

It's the most important, but it's the last priority. Why?

Because if I try to do all that stuff first, I'm going to go broke before I get to any of the other stuff.

I hope you are picking up what I'm putting down.

SECTION III

B.O.S.S. Level
Persuasion

HOW TO BECOME THE PERSON WHO CAN DO THE THING

All human beings have a superpower. In fact, all of us have the *same* superpower, but we don't all know how to use it.

Do you remember the show from the '80s called *The Greatest American Hero*? This guy finds a superhero suit, puts it on, and it gives him the ability to fly—it gives him superhuman strength, but he's lost the instructions. So he has these superpowers, but he doesn't know how to use them. He's trying to save the day and he's flying, and every time he tries to land, he comes crashing through a wall or something.

If you have a superpower and you don't know how to use it, then you're going to end up like The Greatest American Hero. You may know how to take off, but you're not going to land very well. Does that make sense?

So my job is to teach you how to tap into and access your greatest superpower. The superpower that you have, that all of us have, is expectation. But we don't know how to use it for the outcomes we desire. We use our greatest superpower against ourselves by expecting outcomes we don't desire.

You've got to learn to only expect outcomes you desire.

You may be thinking, *I like the idea of that, but how do I do that?*

We are going to get to that, but the first thing I'm going to show you is how to tap into your superpower. When you tap into your superpower and use it for outcomes you desire, you can unlock all of the opportunities available to you in your life.

Your greatest superpower is expectation.

Now, say it out loud. Put your hand over your heart and say out loud: *My greatest superpower is expectation.*

That's powerful. It's so much more powerful than you believe right now.

I'm going to tell you something. Most people believe more in their doubts than they do in their beliefs. In fact, most people believe their doubts and doubt their beliefs.

Are you getting this?

What you've got to learn to do is to believe your beliefs and doubt your doubts.

What's really tragic is that as we go through the miseducation, misdirectional system, also known as government indoctrination camps, they tell us what to think, but nobody teaches us *how* to think, because when you learn how to think, no one can stop you.

Let me ask you this: What would you attempt if you knew you could not fail?

Everything your heart desires, right?

Right.

So, if you knew you could not fail—and be completely honest— if you knew the next thing you were going to work on was going to work, and you knew 100% without any doubt at all, how much of your effort, time, energy, and money would you put into it?

All of it, right?

All of it.

Isn't that interesting? If that's the truth, then the real reason you've not succeeded is that you don't believe what you're working on is going to work. That's the real reason. The thing that's holding you back is your beliefs.

When a fact enters your head, your focus builds a frame around it. That frame is going to cause you to have this thing called belief.

What people don't realize about belief is this:

Faith and doubt are both belief.

Did you pick up what I just put down?

Faith and doubt are two sides of the same coin of belief.

Belief is a two-sided coin. Heads, faith. Tails, doubt.

Doubt is belief in the outcomes I don't desire. Faith is belief in the outcomes I do desire.

Here's what happens: We tell ourselves we're going to do things that we know we have no intention of doing because we already believe it's not going to work. So we sabotage our success.

Fact → Focus → Feeling → Function

We get these beliefs about facts in our heads.

Your fact could be a situation. It could be a circumstance. It could be an incident. It could be whatever. When you look at that fact, you assign a value to it. You assume it means something, you give it context, and you focus on it.

The fact is not what's important.

It could be: *I'm rich, I'm broke. I've got a job, I don't have a job. I have money, I don't have money.*

None of that matters.

Here's what matters: Your focus.

Focus creates a frame.

What your focus tells you about that fact is what matters. The frame that you put around facts will determine which side of the belief-coin you're operating from—whether it's faith or doubt.

And here's what's really interesting ... There's only one thing that moves people.

This is important, so pay attention.

There's only one reason people ever do anything.

There's one reason people buy. There's one reason people don't buy.

There's one reason people start a business and they make it succeed.

There's one reason people start a business and they don't make it succeed.

Everything that everybody does, they do for one reason.

Would you like to know what that reason is?

That reason is …

Because they *feel* like it.

People do what they do because they feel like it.

People don't do what they don't do because they don't feel like it.

It's true.

You say, *Myron, it can't be that simple.*

Now, if you want something complicated, you are going to have to find somebody else. Because the truth is always simple. It's lies that are complicated.

And I'm telling you, when people buy from you, they buy from you for one reason, and one reason only: because they *feel* like buying from you.

Now, there are some things that go into helping them feel like it, but they buy from you because they feel like it. When they don't buy from you, it's because they don't feel like it.

When you take action in the direction of your dreams, you do it because you feel like it. When you don't take action in the direction of your dreams, you don't do it because you don't feel like it.

Belief is a traveling salesman.

The belief that you have in your head (the fact that you focus on) always comes down and manifests in your heart as a feeling. That feeling is either going to empower you to move or it's going to disempower you from moving.

See, I don't have to use willpower to make myself exercise. I have to use willpower to make myself *feel* like exercising. And there's a difference. Because when I feel like exercising, I'm going to exercise. When I feel like eating the chocolate cake, though, I'm going to eat the chocolate cake.

And so, the question is, how do I get myself to feel like doing the things that are in my best interest, and how do I get myself not to feel like doing the things that are not in my best interest?

When the faith side of the belief-coin migrates down to the heart, it manifests itself as anticipation.

Anticipation is a feeling that empowers action.

Anticipation is a feeling that infuses energy.

Can you remember when you were a little child on Christmas Eve and you knew what you were getting the next day? What was the hardest thing in the world to do? Go to sleep, right? Why is that? It's because your expectation and the anticipation of that next day (and the presents you were getting) charged you up so much, you couldn't sleep.

Have you ever gotten a business idea, started working on it, and the next thing you know, 13 hours have gone by? Where'd the time go? You got infused by that idea and your anticipation of this thing working.

On the other side of the belief-coin, you have doubt. That belief manifests as a feeling of anxiety in your heart. When you have a feeling of anxiety, it is paralyzing.

Anxiety is the thief of your dreams.

Everything in your life that you desire—anything you've been working toward that you don't have right now—you don't have because of anxiety. People say, *But I have a fear of failure.* You don't have a fear of failure. You have anxiety over failure. They're not the same thing. They feel similar, but they're not the same.

The reason anxiety and fear are not the same is that fear is caution over a real and present danger; whereas, anxiety is caution over a future *imagined* danger.

You're so worried about the webinar not working that you don't ever launch the webinar. Worrying about it not working makes it not work because you won't work on it.

You've got to learn to overcome anxiety! Because as I said before, "Anxiety is the thief of your dreams!"

Anxiety is often the result of asking the wrong questions.

The main wrong question that people ask that keeps them stuck like Chuck in a pickup truck is: "What if it doesn't work?" That is such a terrible question that it can only have a terrible answer! Here's what you don't understand: *Ask and you shall receive.*

So if you ask the wrong question, guess what you're going to receive?

The wrong answer.

A much better question to ask is this: "How awesome is this going to be when it works?"

Asking better questions will cause you to start creating anticipation instead of anxiety. Anticipation is the energy you get when the outcome you expect is desirable to you. Anxiety is the opposite and must be avoided at all costs!

What does anxiety look like? It looks like me getting into my Bentley in my driveway—12-cylinder engine, 700-horsepower, with a tank full of gas ... What can happen when I rev up my engine in the driveway but never put it in drive?

Two things: I can either blow the engine or run out of gas. And that's the same thing that happens in entrepreneurs' lives. They're wasting all this energy revving up their emotions. Sadly, sometimes it results in blowing their engine in the form of a stroke or heart attack. Other times it just drains them of the energy to act, and they procrastinate until the opportunity is gone.

This is why the stuff you're working on isn't working. It's because you're fighting yourself. It doesn't make sense to desire one thing and believe in the opposite.

Have you ever heard the saying, "Worrying about something makes it happen?" The reason worrying about it makes it happen is that worrying about it robs you of the energy to do the thing that makes it not happen.

Anxiety is *wasting* present energy on a future undesirable outcome.

Anticipation is *gaining* present energy from a future desirable outcome.

These feelings of anxiety in your heart are also traveling salesmen, and they manifest as a function in your hand: Fact → Focus → Feeling → Function.

Let's explore this idea of energy for a minute. I want you to understand something:

Everything is energy.

Energy is neither created nor destroyed, it just changes form. Now, that's a physics principle. May I give you another physics principle?

No high-energy result will ever flow to a low-energy source.

By the way, wealth is a high-energy result, which means unless you bring all the energy you've got to everything you do, you have no hope whatsoever of creating wealth.

What you've got to do is you've got to *become* a high-energy source.

Raise your right hand and say this out loud:

I will, for the rest of my life, be a high-energy source.

Now say this out loud:

Anything I tell myself about a future outcome, I made it up.

Did you catch that?

Anything you tell yourself about a future outcome, you made it up.

When we get into our cars to leave where we've been, we say: *Well, I'm going home.*

What we really mean is we *intend* to go home, but the reality is, do we know for sure we're going to make it home?

No, but do we really *believe* we're going to make it home?

Yes.

Because if we didn't, we wouldn't leave. We'd stay there.

Hang in there with me now.

So I borrow energy ... I don't even borrow it, I just grab some energy from the future.

And when I grab some energy from the future and I use that energy from the future to take action in the present, that makes that future thing manifest.

So instead of asking what if it doesn't work, I ask myself better questions. I ask:

- How awesome is this going to be when it works?

- How amazing is my life going to be when this works?

- How awesome is it going to be when my funnel's making me $100,000 a month or $100,000 a day for that matter?

And I tell myself: *When I build this business, it's going to be great.*

But we don't ask ourselves empowering questions, and we wonder why we go through life with disempowering answers.

For example, people say, "Myron, are you worried about the hurricane?"

And I think, *Not in the slightest.*

"Myron, are you ready for the hurricane?"

Sure, whatever that means.

People somehow think it helps to get themselves all revved up about this future event that's supposed to be happening. I'm not saying the hurricane's not real. The hurricane's obviously real. The hurricane is going to hit Florida. But how much of the wind and water can I stop by worrying about it?

Exactly how much?

Not a bit.

So why should I worry about it? Worrying is a waste of energy. Why not put my energy into something that's going to make my life better and give me the ability to make other people's lives better?

You've got to learn how to master your beliefs.

At this point, you may be wondering, *But how do I master my beliefs, Myron?*

Well, I'm going to ask you to participate in an exercise that will help illustrate how your facts (beliefs) get framed by your focus, how that manifests as your feelings, and why your feelings are the reason for your function (actions).

Did you know that you can hide a $100 bill behind a penny? Even though a $100 bill is worth 10,000 times more and is probably 44 times larger than a penny, you can hide it behind the penny without balling it up. Try it.

Hold a $100 bill (or any amount you have handy) in your right hand with your arm outstretched. Now, hold the penny with your left hand, but hold it just an inch or so from your right eye while you close your left eye.

155

What happened?

When your fortune is far enough away from you, and your lack is close enough to you, not only can you not see your fortune—which is within arm's reach—you can't even clearly see what's surrounding you.

In fact, when a penny is that close to your eye, you can't tell it's a penny. It doesn't look like a penny. When your lack is that close to your eye, it doesn't look like lack. You know what it looks like? It looks like *just the way things are.*

So many of us stay stuck our whole lives because we let things that we lack—things that are as insignificant as a penny—keep us from our destiny.

I'm about to bring it in. Are you ready for things to get real? Roll with me here.

You've got to start making up stories that serve you.

For example, if I tell myself that other people love to pay me, does that mean they really love to pay me?

Maybe, maybe not.

The truth is, I don't know.

If I tell myself that people don't love to pay me, is that true?

Maybe, maybe not.

I don't know.

But if I'm going to make up a story about my future, I might as well make up a story that does me good instead of making up a story that does me harm.

Does that make sense?

I like to believe that since I'm making up a story about other people and I don't know them anyway, I might as well make up a story that serves me instead of a story that doesn't serve me.

Now, do you believe that other people love to pay you?

Believing other people love to pay you is as easy as believing they don't love to pay you. Believing they love to pay you is a good belief. I want you to own that belief for the rest of your life.

Here is another thing I want you to remember: When you've got an opportunity to make your life better—a lot better—and it's only going to take a little bit of time and it costs a little bit of money by comparison, you've got to have a sense of urgency and you've got to act now.

When?

Now.

You deserve to get to the place where money is not an emotional crisis conversation for you. It's just money.

You think you have all this time with the people that you love, and you figure you're going to have all this time to make your life work. It is now o'clock. It is time to get in the game to win the game.

If you find yourself thinking, *I don't have the money …*

How much longer do you want that to be your story? As a full-grown man or a full-grown woman, you don't have the money? I'm going to tell you something. There are a lot of things in my life I didn't have the money for. There were times I didn't have the money, and guess what I did. I figured it out.

I made a decision and figured it out, and that's what you deserve to do. But more important than that, that's what your family deserves for you to do.

I don't need any more money. So, why am I creating more wealth? So I can give it away. I can give it to my children and my grandchildren. I'm not creating wealth for myself. I don't need another car, I don't need another house. It's all for the legacy.

You deserve to live your life with your family. My kids grew up with mom and dad both at home, and when we went somewhere, we all went. How cool is that? You deserve that kind of lifestyle. Wealth gives you choices, and you deserve choices.

Make a decision.

When you make a decision, you cut yourself off from every other possibility.

If you have not yet become the person who can do the thing, the first thing you need to do is "decide" to do it, which is not the same as "choose" to do it.

The word "choose" means to pick one. The word "decide" is compound: "de-" means "of" or "from," and "-cide" means "to cut."

When you "decide," you cut yourself off from all other possibilities.

A lot of people make a choice, but they think they are making a decision.

Decisions create confidence.

What does that mean?

The root word of confidence is the word confide. The word confide means to trust. The reason people don't have confidence is that they cannot confide in themselves. They don't trust themselves.

Why don't people trust themselves?

Because they've broken their word to themselves so many times they can't believe a word they say! Every time you let yourself off the hook, you are breaking a covenant with yourself.

Understand that a covenant is an agreement between two or more individuals based upon mutual love and trust.

When you make a covenant with someone, you are swearing on your own existence to keep that promise, and you're saying, "I would rather die in honor and keep my word than to live in dishonor and break my promise."

When you learn to make decisions, which in reality are covenants with yourself, you will begin to trust yourself, and you will have the confidence to go out and become the person who can do the thing and then have the stuff.

People ask: *What should I do?* If I tell you what to do, you're not going to do it until you become the person who can do it.

We don't send our two-year-old granddaughter to her room to clean it. She has not yet become the person who can do that. Make sense?

Did you know that the biggest challenge you have in doing whatever it is you want to do with your business—whether it be growing it to $1 million, $10 million, $20 million, $100 million, or whatever your goal is—the biggest problem you have is that you have not yet become the person who can do it.

And, unfortunately, you've been programmed by a system that is designed to program you to fail. By fail, I mean quit working toward your goals.

You'll do something for 15 minutes or 15 days or 15 weeks or 15 months, and when it doesn't produce the result you thought it should produce, you say it didn't work.

I have good news for you.

There's no such thing as work that doesn't work.

All work works, but work is a two-sided coin. Heads: The side where *you're working on it*. Tails: The side where *it's working on you*. When the side "you're working on" seems like it's not working, that's when the part that's "working on you" does its best work.

What happens when you start doing something that feels to you like it's not working?

Let's say you did a presentation and you thought the objective was to make a sale. But what you didn't understand was that the presentation's job was to turn you into a good presenter. So you do the presentation once, and because you didn't make any sales and you thought that was the objective, you don't do it again.

You end up protecting yourself from the very activity—from the only activity—that can produce the result you desire. You get out of the game. You check yourself out.

And what happens when you check yourself out? You lose what little momentum you had after you got started.

You can fight against the laws of nature all you want, you just can't win.

People say: *But I don't believe in gravity.* That's okay. Gravity doesn't need you to believe in it. And guess what? Neither does momentum.

Momentum is a physics principle that says an object in motion will continue in motion; it will pick up speed and velocity until or unless it is acted upon by an outside force.

So, when you do something that feels like it's not working and you don't do it again, you overcome your momentum and you recreate inertia.

Inertia is a physics principle that says an object at rest will remain at rest until or unless it's acted upon by an outside force.

If you have momentum and you're doing something, but it feels like it's not working, trust me, it's working.

It may not be working *for* you, but it's working *on* you.

Sometimes when things work for you a lot, they don't work on you nearly as much.

I know you want it to work for you, but you're better off when it works on you because when you become the person who can do the thing repeatedly, then it doesn't matter what happens.

It doesn't matter if Facebook takes away your Facebook page.

It doesn't matter if the IRS sends you a million-dollar bill.

It doesn't matter if something interrupts your business or the marketplace changes.

It doesn't matter because you've become the person who can do the thing.

The most important work I ever do is the work I do on me.

Why?

Because that's the way God set it up from the beginning.

In the beginning, God created this platform for us to operate in as human beings. It governs our experience of life.

You say: *I don't believe in God.* That's alright. He's gonna be alright. His feelings ain't hurt. He's gonna be okay.

Here is why all this is important.

Because making more of the wrong moves doesn't make you more *rich*; it just makes you more *tired*. A lot of people have been programmed to believe that "working hard" is the solution. But working hard is only the solution if you're working hard on the thing that's going to produce the biggest outcome.

A lot of people also make the mistake of thinking that work is something God gave man as a punishment for sin. Not true. Work is something God gave man because man was created in the image of God.

Before God created man, he created the heavens and the earth. When I first read that in scripture, I wondered, *Why would he create the heavens and the earth?*

The only answer I've been able to find is that he is creative; therefore, it is his nature to create.

That means:

The first thing the Bible tells us about God is that God is creative.

The first thing God tells man about man is that he created us in his image, which means he created us to create stuff and he made us to make stuff.

God put the work in the world for the man to do before he put the man in the world to do the work. That means …

Business is a good idea because business is a God idea.

When you believe that you are created in the image of someone whose nature is to create, and you discover your purpose at the intersection of your passion and your proficiency, your super-power of expectation will empower you to build and scale the business of your dreams.

CONCLUSION
AND NEXT STEPS

First and foremost, allow me to congratulate you on finishing this book. It is a very rare person indeed who starts to read a book of his/her own volition, especially on how to scale a business. As the saying goes, "It's the start that stops most people." Congratulations for not letting the start stop you.

With so few people who will even begin a book to make their lives better, it is a much smaller number who will read the book to its end. Ultimately, I hope and trust that you will take it a step further and become the person who implements what you've read to the point of mastery!

As an entrepreneur or aspiring entrepreneur, you will more than likely find yourself stuck in one of two categories. If you're in category number 1, you're stuck generating less than $20,000 per month in revenue. If this is where you find yourself, your course of action will be a simple one …

You must learn and master the four pillars that can grow a business. You must master lead generation, lead conversion, customer ascension, and customer retention. You can learn to master these four moves through trial and error, or you can allow me and my team to assist you on this journey and potentially shave years off the learning curve.

If you would like us to assist you in scaling your business to $20,000 per month and beyond, register as a VIP for the Make More Offers Challenge. At the time of this writing, we run a live challenge every month. However, this will not always be the case.

You can register for the challenge at the website below. The General Admission is currently $97 and the VIP Experience is $297. General Admission attendees get to watch the challenge live in a Facebook Group and VIPs meet me live for one hour per day for five days to get their individual questions answered via a Zoom meeting. Go to the website below to register for the challenge:

MakeMoreOffersChallenge.com

If you're in category number 2, you're an entrepreneur who is stuck between $20,000 and $100,000 per month in revenue. If that's where you find yourself right now, we can help.

We have a mastermind of extremely high-level entrepreneurs, many of whom were stuck between $20,000 and $100,000 per month in revenue. We've helped many of them have $100,000 to $900,000 days. We've even helped some of our clients scale their business to the point where they generate $1 million or more in a single day.

While it's obvious that neither I nor anyone else can guarantee you these results (or any results for that matter), I think we can agree that you increase your chances of these kinds of results if you are in an environment where they are passionately pursued and achieved.

If you would like to have some guidance and direction on the way to your big goals, we would be honored to assist you on this journey. I have created a coaching mastermind in which I teach my clients the business model of King Solomon (who, if he were alive today, would be a multi-trillionaire). When my students apply these principles to their businesses, they experience exponential growth, both personally and professionally.

If you'd like to know more about this program and see if you qualify, go to the website below to apply and schedule a call. I can't promise you that you will be accepted. We are only allowing 100 people in this mastermind at a time and most clients renew every year. They know if they don't renew, they will never be allowed back in. To apply for King Solomon's Wisdom Inner Circle, go here:

KingSolomonsCircle.com

CONTACT AND CONNECT

Skillionaire Enterprises LLC

connect@myrongolden.com

717-978-0201

 @myrongolden

 @themyrongolden

 /MyronGolden

FREE RESOURCES

Below you will find a list of free resources that will help you elevate your life and your business acumen.

Find my free *Bible Success Secrets* podcast using any podcast app or visit:

biblesuccesssecrets.libsyn.com

Join the weekly Bible Success Secrets study group on Facebook:

facebook.com/groups/biblesuccesssecrets

Watch Myron Golden on YouTube:

youtube.com/myrongolden

Follow Myron Golden on Instagram:

instagram.com/myrongolden

ACKNOWLEDGMENTS

As you are reading the pages of this book, I want you to know that even though I am the author of this book, there are so many more people who were absolutely essential to the creation of the manuscript.

I want to thank my wife Tonie for being my greatest supporter. I want to thank my son Anthony, my daughter Deedee, and my son-in-law John Breski for being my greatest accountability partners. I want to thank my granddaughter Ari for being my greatest inspiration and reward all at the same time.

I want to thank Russell Brunson, not only for writing the foreword to this book, but also for being the right business coach for me at one of the most critical times in my business career. Thank you, Russell, for your insight, advice, example, and for creating one of the greatest networks of entrepreneurs I have ever been a part of.

I want to thank Lori Lynn, my editor, who was the genius architect who assembled my thoughts and concepts into a manuscript that is organized and readable. I also want to thank Lori and her team—especially Shelby Rawson, Mary Rembert, Kathy Haskins, and Shanda Trofe—for understanding my mission with this book and making sure that mission didn't get lost in technical minutia.

I want to thank Lorrinda Michieka, my VP of Operations, for managing this project as well as almost every other project in my business.

I want to thank Laura Balbo who came in at the eleventh hour and provided support for me to complete this book.

I want to thank Ariel Elise, who is the brilliant developer of my brand concept as well as our Director of Brand Strategy and Marketing. Thank you for making sure the book represented the brand with excellence in the marketplace.

I want to thank Tamia Scarlett for her work on the caricature illustrations in this book.

I want to thank all of the people who contributed to this book in the form of proofreaders, illustrators, and designers. This work wouldn't be the same without all of your hard work, loyalty, and dedication.

Last but not least, I want to thank you for taking the time to read this book and I want to let you know that I trust you to take the concepts you've learned in this book to go and change the world in your own unique way.

ABOUT THE AUTHOR

Myron Golden, Ph.D., teaches everyday people to become wealthy by helping them see the value in the skills and resources they already have but have been undervaluing.

A coveted speaker in business and marketing circles, he travels and speaks internationally, sharing his timeless wisdom.

The author of several books on the subjects of business and finance, Myron has assisted his clients in building businesses that do as much as $10 million per year in revenue.

One of his superpowers is being able to make millionaires into multimillionaires. His favorite way to do that is through a quantum leap.

His book *From The Trash Man to The Cash Man: How Anyone Can Get Rich Starting from Anywhere* sold over 155,000 copies in the first two years of being in print. His top three most recommended books are the Holy Bible, *You²* by Price Pritchett, Ph.D., and *The Oracle* by Rabbi Jonathan Cahn.

Born in a segregated hospital in Tampa, Florida, he contracted polio as an infant. As a result, he walks with a limp and wears a brace on his left leg, but he also holds a black belt in karate.

He currently resides in Tampa, Florida, with his beautiful wife Tonie. He has two adult children, DeeDee and Anthony, and one son, Adam, who lost his life in a car accident when he was 20 years old.

Besides speaking from stage and playing golf as often as possible, his favorite thing in the world to do is play with his grandbaby Ari Isabella.

B.O.S.S.
CHALLENGE

Are you up for the greatest
challenge of your life?

MakeMoreOffersChallenge.com